ON WORSHIP

ON WORSHIP

A SHORT GUIDE TO UNDERSTANDING, PARTICIPATING IN, AND LEADING CORPORATE WORSHIP

H.B. CHARLES JR.

MOODY PUBLISHERS
CHICAGO

Unless otherwise indicated, Scripture quotations are from the *ESV® Bible (The Holy Bible, English Standard Version®)*, Copyright © 2001 by Crossway, a publishing ministry of Good News Publishers. Used by permission. All rights reserved.

Scripture quotations marked NKJV are taken from the New King James Version. Copyright © 1982 by Thomas Nelson. Used by permission. All rights reserved.

All emphasis in Scripture has been added.

Some of this material has been used previously on the author's blog, https://hbcharlesjr.com/.

Edited by Cheryl Molin
Interior design: Ragont Design
Cover design: Erik M. Peterson
Author photo: Derrick Wilson

All websites and phone numbers listed herein are accurate at the time of publication but may change in the future or cease to exist. The listing of website references and resources does not imply publisher endorsement of the site's entire contents. Groups and organizations are listed for informational purposes, and listing does not imply publisher endorsement of their activities.

Library of Congress Cataloging-in-Publication Data

Names: Charles, H. B., author.
Title: On worship : a short guide to understanding, participating in, and
  leading corporate worship / H.B. Charles, Jr.
Description: Chicago : Moody Publishers, [2022] | Includes bibliographical
  references. | Summary: "On Worship casts a vision for the biblical
  principles and practices of worship. Pastors and leaders will learn what
  the Bible teaches about worship and why it is so important to be
  thoughtful about its practices. You'll also learn how to think
  practically through preparing and executing corporate worship services
  so that you can lead your congregation to worship wholeheartedly in
  spirit and truth"-- Provided by publisher.
Identifiers: LCCN 2022000958 (print) | LCCN 2022000959 (ebook) | ISBN
  9780802419941 (paperback) | ISBN 9780802498861 (ebook)
Subjects: LCSH: Public worship. | BISAC: RELIGION / Christian Rituals &
  Practice / Worship & Liturgy | RELIGION / Christian Ministry / Pastoral
  Resources
Classification: LCC BV15 .C4155 2022 (print) | LCC BV15 (ebook) | DDC
  264--dc23/eng/20220128
LC record available at https://lccn.loc.gov/2022000958
LC ebook record available at https://lccn.loc.gov/2022000959

Originally delivered by fleets of horse-drawn wagons, the affordable paperbacks from D. L. Moody's publishing house resourced the church and served everyday people. Now, after more than 125 years of publishing and ministry, Moody Publishers' mission remains the same—even if our delivery systems have changed a bit. For more information on other books (and resources) created from a biblical perspective, go to www.moodypublishers.com or write to:

Moody Publishers
820 N. LaSalle Boulevard
Chicago, IL 60610

1 3 5 7 9 10 8 6 4 2

To my father, H.B. Charles Sr.,
and my mother, Ellen L. Charles,
who taught me to live, serve, and worship
to the glory of God

CONTENTS

INTRODUCTION

I pitched the idea of writing this book. I thought it would be a book I could write quickly and then move on to other projects. I overestimated myself and underestimated the subject. Worship is not about worship. It is about God. Christianity is truth-driven. Therefore, preaching and teaching are essential to our faith. But the goal of our pursuit of truth is proper worship, not merely proper understanding. When done correctly, theology leads to doxology.

To be honest, this little book was hard to write because of the breadth of the subject and its depth. I have written previously on preaching and pastoring. I believe I have a biblical philosophy of these ministry subjects. After more than thirty years of experience in pastoring a church and preaching each week, I feel comfortable writing about those subjects. Who, truly, is competent to write about worship? And if writers feel confident that worship is a subject they have thoroughly mastered, should we be reading what they think?

I grew up in church. My father was the pastor, and my mother was the minister of music. I was at church every time the doors were open. And believe me, they were open a lot. The cool kids sat in the overflow section. I sat right up front, near the deacons, in front of the musical instruments. At an early age, I accepted that I had no choice but to attend church and participate in the services. So I tried to make the most of my sentence by paying attention to what was going on. The grace of the Lord Jesus Christ gripped my heart and has not let me go.

Throughout my life, I have participated in countless worship services. The services have always moved my heart. But I did not always understand what we did or why we did it. As a result, much of my spiritual journey has been refining my worship to fit biblical principles. Pastoring for three decades has intensified this process. Many in the church are like me. The details of our stories are different, but for all of us, our upbringing ran ahead of our convictions. Tradition rather than truth governed worship. We had an experience without understanding.

This book is written to help church leaders and members think through biblical principles and practices of worship. *On Worship* is not a theological treatise, biblical study, or comprehensive handbook on worship. (For more thorough treatments of the subject, check out the reading suggestions at the end of this book.) Like my previous books, *On Preaching* and *On Pastoring*, this book is more like a compass than a road map. It seeks to point you in the right direction.

The two previous books were written directly to pastors. However, I have written this book in hopes that a wider audience will also find it helpful. The chapters are short and the book is divided into three sections. First, we will talk about the what and why of worship. Then we discuss the practice of worship. Finally, I will offer some counsel to those who lead worship. I pray you will find this work beneficial, whether you are a pastor-teacher, worship leader, or lay member. I pray that *On Worship* will help you grow in your understanding, leadership, and offering of worship to the glory of God.

Part 1:

UNDERSTANDING WORSHIP

Chapter 1

>>> ✝ <<<

THE ULTIMATE PRIORITY

A principle of Bible interpretation called the Law of First Mention simply means that clues to understanding a biblical subject are often found in the first time it is mentioned in Scripture. The introductory reference to a subject can teach us a lot about how Scripture views it.

This principle is one reason that the book of Genesis is so vital to biblical theology and Christian doctrine. It is the book of beginnings that addresses matters of origin. Genesis 1–2 records the story of creation. Genesis 3 tells the story of the fall of humanity into sin. As you read into chapter 4, Genesis continues to introduce important firsts in human history: the first sex act, the first pregnancy, the first birth, the first siblings, the first shepherd, the first murder, and the first lie.

This first act of worship teaches the ultimate priority of worship: make sure the Lord is pleased.

In this chapter, I want us to consider another first recorded in Genesis 4: the first offering of worship, which Cain and Abel offered to the Lord. Theirs was probably not the first ever offering of worship in history. Most likely, Adam and Eve offered worship to the Lord and taught their children to do so. But it is the first recorded one. As such, it sets a precedent. This first act of worship teaches the ultimate priority of worship: make sure the Lord is pleased.

The Bible says Adam knew Eve his wife (Gen. 4:1). Eve conceived and gave birth to a son, whom they named Cain. Cain followed in his father's footsteps and worked the ground as a farmer. Eve conceived again and gave birth to Abel, the first of a long line of godly shepherds. After introducing us to Cain and Abel and their respective vocations, Scripture abruptly shifts to the offering of worship they presented to God: "In the course of time Cain brought to the LORD an offering of the fruit of the ground, and Abel also brought of the firstborn of his flock and of their fat portions" (Gen. 4:3–4a).

The report of Cain and Abel's offerings has no obvious agenda. Moses simply reports that both men brought an offering in keeping with their respective vocations. Cain, the farmer, presented an offering from the fruit of the ground. Abel, the shepherd, presented an offering from his flock of sheep. The focus is not on the men or their offerings. The stress is placed on the Lord's response to the two men's offerings: "And the LORD had regard for Abel and his offering, but for Cain and his offering he had no regard" (Gen. 4:4b–5a).

ACCEPTABLE WORSHIP

This first recorded act of worship was definitely not about what Cain and Abel got out of it. Their vocations, resources, or preferences were not considered. It was about whether God was pleased with their offerings. The text is clear that God accepted one offering and not the other. Interestingly, the text ties these brothers to their offerings. The Lord had regard for Abel *and* his offering. But the Lord had no regard for Cain *and* his offering. This is how worship works. You cannot separate how God views you from how God views your worship. "For the LORD sees not as man sees: man looks on the outward appearance, but the LORD looks on the heart" (1 Sam. 16:7b).

Why did God regard Abel and his offering and disregard Cain and his offering? The text does not specify, yet it is the subject of much debate. The most logical reason given is because Cain's offering was not a blood offering. A blood offering would later be legislated by Moses for the atonement of sin. Moreover, blood sacrifices pointed forward to the substitutionary death of Christ. Hebrews 12:24 says we have come to "Jesus, the mediator of a new covenant, and to the sprinkled blood that speaks a better word than the blood of Abel." In the Old Testament, however, God accepted both blood and grain offerings.

Others contend that the problem was the quality of Cain's offering. They claim Cain gave less than his best, while Abel gave from the finest of his flock of sheep. But the text does not suggest that Cain gave the Lord old, rotten, or damaged fruit. For all we know, Cain's offering was from the firstfruits of his field, even as Abel's offering was from the fattest of his flock.

Still others contend that God took issue with the manner of Cain's offering—that his attitude was wrong. That may have been the case. But, again, the text does not tell us what either brother's attitude was as they presented their offerings.

All we know for sure is that one boy presented an offering that pleased the Lord and the other did not. Hebrews 11:4 says: "By faith Abel offered to God a more acceptable sacrifice than Cain, through which he was commended as righteous, God commending him by accepting his gifts. And through his faith, though he died, he still speaks." That does not answer all of our questions, but I believe it makes the point: the priority of true worship is to make sure God is pleased.

After worship on Sunday, a member bluntly said to the pastor, "I did not enjoy the service today." Reciprocating the member's bluntness, the pastor replied, "That's okay. We weren't worshiping you." That response may seem overly harsh. But it is absolutely true. Worshipers constantly need this reminder. Worship is not about us. It is not about our needs, tastes, or preferences.

The worship wars of past decades argued about whether worship should focus on "seekers" or the saints. Ultimately, both sides were wrong. God is the target audience of worship. Paul exulted, "For from him and through him and to him are all things. To him be glory forever. Amen" (Rom. 11:36). All things find their source, being, and purpose in God alone. Thus, God alone deserves the glory in all things. The only way we have the right to receive glory is if anything is from us, through us, or to us. We got here too late and will leave too early to claim any share in divine glory. The ultimate priority of true worship is that the Lord is pleased.

THE PERSON OF WORSHIP

In the Sermon on the Mount (Matt. 5–7), Jesus taught that citizenship in the kingdom of heaven requires righteousness, not religiosity. Yet in Matthew 6, Jesus taught how righteous people should do religious stuff. Jesus gave instructions about the most Godward of acts: giving, prayer, and fasting (Matt. 6:1–18). He warned that we must be careful not to do these things to be seen by people. The consequence of offering worship for human consumption is severe: "You have already received your reward" (see v. 16). Jesus repeatedly admonishes us to do acts of worship before God in private. These admonitions do not forbid public, corporate acts of worship.

They warn us that worship must not become a platform to perform for people. It does not matter what people see, think, or say. It only matters that the Lord is pleased.

More than a century ago, worshipers filled the Plymouth Church in Brooklyn one Sunday to hear its famous pastor, Henry Ward Beecher. They were disappointed to find that Henry's less prominent brother, Thomas K. Beecher, filled the pulpit that day. People began to get up and walk out. As many headed for the doors, Thomas stood in the pulpit and announced, "All those who came here this morning to worship Henry Ward Beecher may withdraw from the church, but all who came to worship God may remain." Jolted to their senses, chastised worshipers returned to their pews.[1]

May we never forget that we gather not to please ourselves or to please others. We worship to please the Lord. The anonymous author of Hebrews issued this call to worship: "Through him then let us continually offer up a sacrifice of praise to God, that is, the fruit of lips that acknowledge his name. Do not neglect to do good and to share what you have, for such sacrifices are pleasing to God" (Heb. 13:15–16).

Make sure the Lord is pleased with your life.

Make sure the Lord is pleased with your offering.

Make sure the Lord is pleased with your motives.

Make sure the Lord is pleased with your attitude.

Make sure the Lord is pleased with your relationships.

Chapter 2

✝

HOW TO WORSHIP GOD

In the first word of the Ten Commandments, God commanded His people to worship Him exclusively: "You shall have no other gods before me" (Ex. 20:3). The second word is linked to the first:

> "You shall not make for yourself a carved image, or any likeness of anything that is in heaven above, or that is in the earth beneath, or that is in the water under the earth. You shall not bow down to them or serve them, for I the Lord your God am a jealous God, visiting the iniquity of the fathers on the children to the third and fourth generation of those who hate me, but showing steadfast love to thousands of those who love me and keep my commandments." (Ex. 20:4–6)

There is some disagreement about how the Ten Commandments should be numbered. Roman Catholics and Lutherans read the first and second commandments as one commandment. To keep ten commandments, they call the preamble (Ex. 20:2) a commandment or divide the tenth commandment (Ex. 20:17) into two parts.

Exodus 20:3 and 4–6 record two different commands. They are

two different sides of the same coin. The first commandment is about the proper object of worship. The second commandment is about the proper mode of worship. The first commandment addresses orthodoxy (right belief). The second commandment addresses orthopraxy (right practice). The first commandment tells us whom to worship. The second commandment tells us how to worship. God says, "Worship Me alone." Then God says, "Worship Me this way." How we worship matters to God.

> **When the children of Israel danced around the golden calf, the Lord did not respond, "Look how sincere they are!"**

The second commandment does not prohibit God's people from being artistic. The Lord will instruct Moses to have artisans construct the ark of the covenant with artistic elements. The Spirit of God would inspire and empower men to creatively build the tabernacle. This is not a categorical prohibition against carved images. The Lord's concern here is liturgical, not artistic. We must not make carved images for worship.

The second commandment warns us how misguided sincerity can be. When the children of Israel danced around the golden calf, the Lord did not respond, "Look how sincere they are!" The Lord became so angry that only the passionate intercession of Moses saved their lives. God demands proper worship.

WORSHIP GOD ON HIS TERMS

It is remarkable that the first commandment was necessary. After delivering the children of Israel from Egypt, God still needed to instruct His people not to worship false idols. The second commandment is a natural progression from the first. God disabuses His people of the assumption that it does not matter how we worship, as long as we worship the right God. Redeemed people can still offer unacceptable worship if it is not on God's terms.

God cannot be controlled. That is what happens with carved images. A symbol makes visible what is invisible and tangible what is intangible. In so doing, the reality behind the symbol is tamed, controlled, and neutered. Why do you think there is so much controversy over the American flag? It is a symbol that points to a reality. How one treats the symbol is a statement of what one thinks about the reality it represents.

The Babylonians had to carry their gods away on wagons to flee Cyrus of Persia. Yet the Lord reminded the house of Israel that He carried them since birth and will continue to carry them and save them (Isa. 46:3–4). This is why God forbids carved images. God carries us and refuses to be put in a position where we try to carry Him.

This second word may seem irrelevant. But we need this commandment today. Many Western contemporary Christians are ancient Hebrew idolaters in disguise. We make symbols for God; then we make gods of our symbols. We profess to worship the God of Abraham, Isaac, Jacob, Jesus, and the church. We actually worship the God of our cause, understanding, experience, race, nation, comfort, and success.

WORSHIP GOD BY DIVINE REVELATION

There are two primary ways finite man seeks to know the infinite God: by imagination or revelation. Seeking to know God by trying to imagine who He is does not work. The second commandment prohibits any attempts to shape an image of God according to who or what we think God is. Habakkuk asked, "What profit is an idol when its maker has shaped it, a metal image, a teacher of lies? For its maker trusts in his own creation when he makes speechless idols!" (Hab. 2:18). The only way to know God is by revelation. We cannot imagine the nature, character, attributes, purpose, or glory of God. God must reveal Himself to us.

In a general sense, God reveals Himself in the created world. Creation advertises its Creator (Ps. 19:1). Heaven and earth proclaim the reality of God. But creation cannot declare the name of God. To know God personally, we need special revelation. God has personally revealed Himself to us in the Bible (2 Tim. 3:16). We must worship God on the basis of His revelation of Himself to us. God-pleasing worship is Word-driven worship.

When Israel met with God for the first time, they heard a voice but saw no image (Deut. 4:11–12). Moses reminded Israel of this to prepare them for the non-appearance of God. In the days to come, Israel's worship would not be in video format. There would only be audio. They would have CDs to listen to, not DVDs to watch (Deut. 4:15–18). Worship is not about images to see. It is about words to hear. True worship is Word-based, Word-saturated, and Word-driven. We are to sing the Word, read the Word, pray the Word, preach the Word, and see the Word.

WORSHIP GOD THROUGH JESUS CHRIST

God commands us not to make any carved images in the likeness of anything in heaven, on earth, or in the sea. Those who make images of God mar the image of God. What is the image of God? Genesis 1:26–27 says, "Then God said, 'Let us make man in our image, after our likeness . . . ' So God created man in his own image, in the image of God he created him; male and female he created them."

We are the image of God. This does not mean we have physical attributes that represent God: God is spirit (John 4:24). It means that God has given us personhood—mind, will, and emotions. We are free moral agents who can choose between good and evil, right and wrong, truth and error. Adam and Eve rebelled against God in the garden of Eden. All of humanity has fallen into sin as a result of our first parents' original sin. Mankind was doomed to live in misery, die in sin, and suffer in hell. But God sent Jesus to save us. The Lord Jesus Christ is "the radiance of the glory of God and the exact imprint of his nature" (Heb. 1:3).

Jesus is God in the flesh. Truly God, truly man. Paul sang, "He is the image of the invisible God, the firstborn of all creation" (Col. 1:15). Paul also said, "For in him the whole fullness of deity dwells bodily" (Col. 2:9). To worship God is to worship Jesus. Christian worship is Christ worship. The Lord should have supremacy in everything we say and do in worship (Col. 1:18).

On the way home from church, a child told her parents she did not want to go to Sunday school anymore. When asked why, she griped, "Because they never do anything new there. Every week it's the same thing. Jesus, Jesus, Jesus." May that little child's complaint be the legitimate critique of our corporate worship services. No one should ever catch us doing something new when they attend our worship services. It should be the same thing every week, every month, every year. Jesus! Jesus! Jesus!

✝

Chapter 3

A HIGH VIEW OF GOD

Isaiah 6 records Isaiah's life-transforming vision of God and subsequent call to prophetic ministry. It is arguably one of the most well-known passages in Isaiah's prophecy. And rightfully so, for it contains the dramatic testimony of a sinful man who had a violent encounter with God and lived to tell it. Isaiah's gaze was lifted above and beyond his physical surroundings. And he received a vision of God that changed his life immediately, completely, and permanently.

God moved Isaiah to record his testimony in Scripture as a spiritually profitable lesson. Isaiah's vision calls us to a high view of God. Though we should not expect to experience Isaiah's supernatural vision, we desperately need the exalted view of God that resulted from Isaiah's vision. We need a high view of God. A. W. Tozer wrote, "The greatest need of the moment is that lighthearted, superficial religionists be struck down with a vision of God high and lifted up, with his train filling the temple."[2]

To worship is to ascribe worth. The legitimacy of worship is based on the worthiness of the object. You do not get

Proper worship requires divine revelation. You must see God as He truly is to worship Him as He deserves and demands. Your view of God is everything!

worship right by focusing on worship. Proper worship requires divine revelation. You must see God as He truly is to worship Him as He deserves and demands. Your view of God is everything!

Jeremiah wrote:

> Thus says the LORD: "Let not the wise man boast in his wisdom, let not the mighty man boast in his might, let not the rich man boast in his riches, but let him who boasts boast in this, that he understands and knows me, that I am the LORD who practices steadfast love, justice, and righteousness in the earth. For in these things I delight, declares the LORD." (Jer. 9:23–24)

Without a proper view of God, you have nothing. Only when you see God properly will everything else be brought into focus.

Isaiah testified, "In the year that King Uzziah died I saw the Lord sitting upon a throne, high and lifted up; and the train of his robe filled the temple" (Isa. 6:1). Isaiah's timestamp is critical to the vision. Uzziah was the tenth king of Judah. He took the throne at the age of sixteen and reigned for fifty-two years. King Uzziah was "marvelously helped" by God (2 Chron. 26:15), which led to political, military, and economic success. But when he became strong, he became proud. His pride led to his downfall. God struck the rebellious king with leprosy, and he died quarantined from the nation he built (2 Chron. 26:21).

In the year Uzziah died, Isaiah saw the Lord sitting on a throne. One way or another, every king, prime minister, president, and dictator will give up power. And when the parade of dethroned rulers is over, God will be where He has always been: sitting on His throne, high and lifted up, with His train filling the temple.

THE GLORY OF GOD

Jesus said, "God is spirit" (John 4:24). Paul said God "dwells in unapproachable light, whom no one has ever seen or can see" (1 Tim. 6:16). John said, "No one has ever seen God" (1 John 4:12). Yet Isaiah says, "I saw the Lord" (Isa. 6:1). Isaiah did not see God's essential nature. He saw a vision of God's sovereign authority (indicated by the fact that the Lord sat on a throne). The prophet declared, "My eyes have seen the King" (Isa. 6:5).

John's gospel presents the rejection of Jesus as the fulfillment of Isaiah 6:10. After quoting the prophet, John wrote, "Isaiah said these things because he saw his glory" (12:41). Isaiah's vision was a Christophany. He received a sneak preview of coming attractions. Before the incarnation of Christ, Isaiah saw the Lord Jesus enthroned in heaven. Here is a hint of the trinitarian nature of Christian worship. You cannot worship God the Father without worshiping God the Son. You cannot worship God the Son without worshiping God the Father.

In Isaiah's vision, he saw the Lord. He also saw the seraphim. These angelic creatures had six wings each. With two wings, they flew. With four wings, they veiled their faces and feet in the presence of God. The posture of the seraphim illustrates the holiness of God. Understandably, a sinful man would feel doomed before God (Isa. 6:5). But the fear of the holy angels declares how holy the Lord is. God is not just set apart from sin. He is set apart from all creation. The angels sang, "Holy, holy, holy is the Lord of hosts" (Isa. 6:3). This antiphonal song declares the infinite holiness of God.

To say that God is holy once is enough.

To say that God is holy twice is emphatic.

To say that God is holy three times is superlative.

God is so holy that our minds cannot comprehend it and our

mouths cannot express it. To say that God is holy is to say that God is God. Holiness is the "Godness" of God. Worship that does not revere the holiness of God is not worship. It is the idolatrous veneration of a god of our own making.

In worshiping the holiness of God, the angels also declared, "The whole earth is full of his glory" (Isa. 6:3). This statement about the glory of God is even more remarkable than the statement about the holiness of God. Check the news. The earth is full of evil, violence, racism, corruption, perversity, and folly. But the angels do not view the world based on the news of the day. They view the world in light of the holiness of God. Because God is God alone, angels rightly declare the earth is filled with the glory of God.

We will never be amazed by grace without beholding the holiness of God.

This holy vision of God brought Isaiah to an end of himself. He lamented, "Woe is me! For I am lost; for I am a man of unclean lips, and I dwell in the midst of a people of unclean lips; for my eyes have seen the King, the Lord of hosts" (Isa. 6:5). When you see God as He truly is, you will see yourself as you are. True worship is transformative. But transformation happens in worship not because that is our goal. We change in worship as we behold the glory of the Lord (2 Cor. 3:18).

THE ALTAR OF GOD

In the middle of Isaiah's vision, the heavenly furniture shifts. The focus on the throne (Isa. 6:1–4) becomes a focus on the altar (Isa. 6:6). Eternal punishment happens when there is a throne without an altar, holiness without grace, guilt without forgiveness. But God is a God of holiness and love. We will never be amazed by grace without beholding the holiness of God. When the vision of

God's holiness convicts us of our sinfulness, we will not need to be pumped and primed to worship. It will be the overflow of glad and grateful hearts that are trophies of grace.

The forgiveness of Isaiah's sin was a work of God's grace. His guilt was taken away; his sin was atoned for. Isaiah had nothing to do with the new beginning he received. God did it all! But that did not mean there was no work for Isaiah to do. After his cleansing, Isaiah overheard a heavenly conversation: "Whom shall I send, and who will go for us?" (Isa. 6:8).

Isaiah was a part of this conversation. He knew that he should have died in his sin. Mercy and grace spared him. Divine forgiveness deserved total devotion. So Isaiah butted in, saying, "Here I am! Send me." Isaiah did not know what the mission would be. (In Isa. 6:9–13, he would find out that it was a difficult assignment.) But that did not matter. A high view of God caused him to conclude that the Lord could never ask too much of him.

What is your view of God?

Chapter 4

THE GOD WHO ORDERS WORSHIP

I love the book of Psalms. It is the most honest book I have ever read. The psalms address all the vicissitudes of life—ups and downs, highs and lows, victory and defeat, joy and sorrow, doubt and confidence. When you get to the end of the psalms, the storms cease, the clouds lift, and the sun shines. As darkness gives way to light, the ultimate priority of life comes into view. This ultimate priority is stated as an imperative: "Praise the Lord!"

This call to worship is two words in Hebrew: *halal*, which means to praise or boast; and *Yaw*, a shortened form of Yahweh. The translation is "Hallelujah," or "Praise the Lord." Psalms 146 to 150 all begin and conclude with this command to praise the Lord. But the imperative of worship is most emphatic in the closing psalm, where we are commanded to praise God thirteen times in six verses. The command to praise God begins every line of Psalm 150 except verse 6a, which says, "Let everything that has breath praise the Lord!"

In Psalm 1, God blesses man.

In Psalm 150, man blesses God.

This closing psalm is so preoccupied with commands to praise the Lord that it virtually ignores the worshipers who receive these commands. Verses 3 to 5 record the most detailed list of musical instruments in Scripture. Yet the worshipers who are to play these instruments are not mentioned. The worshipers are lumped together in verse 6 with every living thing God has created. God is the centerpiece of worship. Sir William Temple said it well: "To worship is to quicken the conscience by the holiness of God, to feed the mind with the truth of God, to purge the imagination by the beauty of God, to open the heart to the love of God, to devote the will to the purpose of God."[3] And God alone orders worship.

GOD ORDERS THE PLACE OF WORSHIP

Psalm 150:1 tells us where to worship God: "Praise the LORD! Praise God in his sanctuary; praise him in his mighty heavens!" "Sanctuary" refers to the holy presence of God that dwelt in the meeting place with Israel. "Mighty heavens" is the expanse of space where the sun, moon, and stars reside. These two poetic phrases teach us the Lord is to be worshiped in all of His creation. Praise the Lord on earth and in heaven. Praise the Lord locally and universally. Praise the Lord in the temple and everywhere else. God is worthy to be praised everywhere.

Psalm 137 is a song of lament by the Jews who were conquered by the Babylonians. They sat by the Euphrates River, hung their musical instruments on the trees, and wept. The Babylonians taunted them to sing praise to God. The Israelites asked, "How shall we sing the LORD's song in a foreign land?" (Ps. 137:4).

The worshipers' devotion to the holy place may be commendable. However, it also reflected a low view of God. There is no strange land to the Lord who is fully present everywhere. And He is to be praised in His sanctuary and His mighty heavens. Praise the Lord wherever you are. Hebrews 13:15 exhorts: "Through him then let us continually offer up a sacrifice of praise to God, that is, the fruit of lips that acknowledge his name." The word *continually* means "through it all." We are to praise God through it all.

GOD ORDERS THE PURPOSE OF WORSHIP

Psalm 150:1 tells us where to worship God. Verse 2 tells us why to worship God: "Praise him for his mighty deeds; praise him according to his excellent greatness!" We worship God because God is worthy of our worship. God demands our praise. But we would still be morally obligated to praise God, even if we were not divinely commanded to do it. God deserves our praise.

God deserves our praise because of His mighty deeds. The ancient Jews who read this psalm immediately thought of God's deliverance, provisions, and faithfulness to Israel. But we must read this Old Testament text with New Testament eyes. God's mightiest deeds were accomplished in the virgin birth, righteous life, atoning death, and glorious resurrection of the Lord Jesus Christ. Paul wrote: "The sting of death is sin, and the power of sin is the law. But thanks be to God, who gives us the victory through our Lord Jesus Christ" (1 Cor. 15:56–57).

God also deserves our praise because of His excellent greatness. Psalm 145:3 declares, "Great is the Lord, and greatly to be praised, and his greatness is unsearchable." God is great. And His greatness is excellent. We are to praise God in a manner that honors the surpassing greatness of His high name. This is what it means to give God the highest praise. It is not biblically correct to say that "Hallelujah" is the highest praise. If that term is the highest praise, then unsaved, sinful, and wicked people can offer the highest praise by merely saying the correct password. You cannot give God the highest praise without it radically transforming your life. God receives the highest praise when those who worship His greatness walk in His greatness.

GOD ORDERS THE PRACTICE OF WORSHIP

Psalm 150:1 tells us where to worship God. Verse 2 tells us why to worship God. Verses 3 to 5 tell us how to worship God: "Praise him with trumpet sound; praise him with lute and harp! Praise him with tambourine and dance; praise him with strings and pipe! Praise him with sounding cymbals; praise him with loud clashing cymbals!" This list of musical instruments emphasizes that worship is meant to please God, not us.

God likes orchestra music. God likes instrumental music. God likes vocal music. God likes beautiful music. God likes loud music. God likes energetic music. God even likes music you can dance to!

Specifically, Psalm 150 teaches us that God likes to be praised with music. God likes orchestra music. God likes instrumental music. God likes vocal music. God likes beautiful music. God likes loud music. God likes energetic music. God even likes music you can dance to! But God does not like all music. The conjunction *with*, used six times in verses 3–5, teaches that music is not worship. It is an accompaniment to worship. The point is not about where or how you should use musical instruments in worship. It is about the implications of them.

You cannot get distracted with a trumpet barking at you.

You cannot play the harp with indifference.

You cannot be sophisticated playing the tambourine and jumping around in a dance.

You cannot get bored in worship with stringed instruments

capturing every note and chord in the world of music.

You cannot go to sleep with someone clanging loud cymbals in your ears.

God lists these musical instruments—from winds to strings to percussions—to call for total praise. We should praise God by all means. Our minds, bodies, voices, talents, emotions, and wills—offer all that we are and all that we have to the Lord as a sacrifice of praise.

GOD ORDERS THE PARTICIPANTS OF WORSHIP

Verse 1 tells us where to worship God. Verse 2 tells us why to worship God. Verses 3 to 5 tell us how to worship God. Verse 6 tells us who should worship God. Now that the auditorium is secured, the occasion is established, and the instruments are prepared, God selects a choir. Verse 6 states the criteria: "Let everything that has breath praise the LORD!" This liberal policy for choir membership makes sense. After all, things that do not have breath praise the Lord. Psalm 148:7–9 says: "Praise the LORD from the earth, you great sea creatures and all deeps, fire and hail, snow and mist, stormy wind fulfilling his word! Mountains and all hills, fruit trees and all cedars!" It is only fitting that God should be praised by everything that breathes.

God's glory fills the universe. His praise should do no less.

God, the Creator and Ruler of the world, deserves the praises of everything and everyone.

God's glory fills the universe. His praise should do no less.

Every living thing should sing praises to the Lord.

Worship should not be confined to church services. While we breathe, we should praise.

We should fill the whole world with the praises of God. Our responsibility to praise God is also our opportunity to praise God. You do not need a large bank account, prestigious job, big house, new car, or fancy clothes to praise God. If you have breath in your body, you have sufficient reason to praise the Lord. The fact that you are still here means God is worthy to be praised!

Chapter 5

✝

SPIRIT-FILLED WORSHIP

Are you filled with the Spirit? Ask any random Christian this question, and there is no telling what kind of answer you will get. The answer may be full of assurance or the response may range anywhere from ignorance to fear, speculation, fanaticism, or indifference.

The filling of the Spirit is one of the most controversial, divisive, and misunderstood ministries of the Holy Spirit to believers. Why is there so much confusion about Spirit-infilling? The problem is twofold. It is the double cause of confusion in any matter of Christian thinking or living: no teaching and wrong teaching. In this chapter, however, I do not want to argue doctrinal theories about being filled with the Spirit. I want to make the point that you must be filled with the Spirit to offer true worship.

Before we go any further, let me clarify a common misconception. Spirit-infilling is *not* about getting more of the Spirit. When Christ saves you, the Holy Spirit takes up residence in your heart immediately, completely, and permanently. Paul wrote, "Anyone who does not have the Spirit of Christ does not belong to him" (Rom. 8:9b).

If you are in Christ, you do not need the Holy Spirit to fall on you. He lives within you! Yet there is a difference between Spirit-indwelling and Spirit-infilling. Imagine buying a brand-new car with all the bells and whistles, but you have to push it around in neutral because you cannot figure out how to start the vehicle. This is how many Christians live, worship, and minister—in their own wisdom, energy, and resources. You will not get far like that. The human spirit fails unless the Holy Spirit fills. It does not have to be that way. You can live in the power of what A. Louis Patterson called "the indwelling presence of the Life-Giver King." But you must be filled with the Spirit.

Many New Testament passages mention being filled with the Spirit. Only one passage explains it. Ephesians 5:18 says, "And do not get drunk with wine, for that is debauchery, but be filled with the Spirit."

The verse begins with a prohibition against drunkenness. Literally, Paul says, "Stop getting drunk with wine." This command means what it says. Christians should not get drunk. Drunkenness contradicts our Christian walk, work, and witness. How does one avoid, resist, or overcome such debauchery?

Be filled with the Spirit.

Stay filled with the Spirit.

Keep being filled with the Spirit.

Being filled with the Spirit is not some spiritual intoxication. Sure, a drunk person is under the influence. And so is a Spirit-filled Christian. But the two realities are antithetical (Acts 2:14–15). An intoxicated person loses control of himself. But the fruit of the Spirit is self-control (Gal. 5:22–23). Let me say it another way. Alcohol is a depressant; Spirit-infilling is a stimulant. Being filled with the Spirit enables you to live obediently, worship sincerely, and serve faithfully.

TWO COMMANDS

Being filled with the Spirit is a Christian duty. The New Testament never instructs Christians to be baptized, indwelt, gifted, sealed, or anointed by the Spirit. These Spirit-graces are the standard equipment of the Christian life. For this standard equipment to function correctly, you must be filled with the Spirit. The Word of God commands us to be filled with the Spirit. Ephesians 5:18 contains two commands. Both carry divine authority. It is just as sinful for Christians not to be filled with the Spirit as it is to be drunk with wine.

Every Christian is commanded to be filled with the Spirit. It is not just for Pentecostals or charismatics. Filling is not just for church leaders, mature Christians, or ministry participants. And it is not just for those who desire it or seek it. Spirit-infilling is all-inclusive. Having told us in Ephesians 5:18 to be filled with the Spirit, Ephesians 5:21–6:9 teaches what it looks like for every Christian wife and husband, child and parent, employee and employer to be filled with the Spirit. Think about that. What would your church be like if every member was filled with the Spirit?

Every Christian is commanded to be filled with the Spirit. It is not just for Pentecostals or charismatics. Filling is not just for church leaders, mature Christians, or ministry participants.

How is a Christian filled with the Spirit? Study this subject, and you will find multiple, contradictory answers to this question. The Bible does not give any formula, process, or technique for being filled with the Spirit. But I do believe there is a biblical answer to this question. It is in Colossians 3, which parallels Ephesians 5. Paul gives the same set of instructions in both passages.

Ephesians 5 begins these instructions by saying, "Be filled with the Spirit" (Eph. 5:18).

Colossians 3 begins these instructions by saying, "Let the word of Christ dwell in you richly" (Col. 3:16).

Put these two verses together, and you find the way to be filled with the Spirit. To be filled with the Spirit of God is to be filled with the Word of God. The Holy Spirit and Scripture are not in conflict. They always work together. If you show me a person whose life is governed by the Word of God, I will show you a person whose life is governed by the Spirit of God.

It is worth noting that no Spirit-filled person in Scripture ever claimed to be filled with the Spirit. The primary work of the Holy Spirit is to exalt the Lord Jesus Christ. Jesus said, "He will bear witness about me" (John 15:26). Jesus also said, "He will glorify me" (John 16:14). The Holy Spirit is the "shy" member of the Trinity. When the Spirit shows up, He never draws attention to Himself. He always puts the spotlight on the Lord Jesus. Likewise, Spirit-filled Christians do not show off how spiritual, gifted, or mature they are. To be filled with the Spirit is to be empty of self.

SPIRITUAL CHARACTERISTICS

What are the characteristics of Spirit-infilling? Paul says Spirit-filled Christians will be "addressing one another in psalms and hymns and spiritual songs, singing and making melody to the Lord with your heart" (Eph. 5:19). I am always blown away when I read these words. I wouldn't believe it if it was not in my Bible in black and white. The first evidence that a Christian is filled with the Spirit is that He will put a song in your heart!

No, being filled with the Spirit will not make you a singer. If you could not sing before you were filled with the Spirit, you still can't sing when you are filled with the Spirit. But you will have a song! And you will not sing to promote yourself. You will sing to build up others. Moreover, you will sing to the Lord.

The Lord is not impressed with your vocal ability. Singing that pleases God must come from a heart that is overflowing with grateful praise: "giving thanks always and for everything to God the Father in the name of our Lord Jesus Christ" (Eph. 5:20). Spirit-filled Christians give thanks unceasingly ("always"). And Spirit-filled Christians give thanks unconditionally ("for everything"). A person who grumbles, complains, and finds fault is not filled with the Spirit. Spirit-filled Christians are thankful people. What a beautiful picture of Christian worship! We are to give thanks to the Father in the name of the Son by the filling of the Spirit.

Paul will unpack how being filled with the Spirit shapes our relationships to others (Eph. 5:21–6:9). But he first described how the Holy Spirit transforms the saints into a worshiping community. A. W. Tozer has been attributed with saying, "If the Holy Spirit was withdrawn from the church today, 95 percent of what we do would go on and no one would know the difference." God forbid! May the Spirit of the Lord be obviously present, actively in charge, and dynamically at work when we gather for worship. And may His presence and power overflow from worship to enable us to be living sacrifices (Rom. 12:1) that glorify God.

Chapter 6

✝

WHY THE CHURCH?

More and more people profess to be "unchurched Christians." This is not a biblical category. Ask Paul, John, or Peter what they think about unchurched Christians, and they would respond, "Why are you calling them Christians if they are not a part of the church?"

The New Testament does not have a vision of the Christian life outside of the church, the local church. Yet many professing Christians seek to be committed to Christ with no commitment to the church. They do not believe in organized religion. They claim the church is full of hypocrites. They do not find the church necessary, supportive, or beneficial. Thus, they follow Christ but forsake the church.

It is wrong.

It is unbiblical.

It is non-Christian.

Though the church is imperfect and some people have experienced church hurt, or they cannot find a faithful, Bible-teaching church, you cannot have a high view of Christ and a low view of the church at the same time. Jesus declared, "On this rock I will build my church, and the gates of hell shall not prevail against it" (Matt. 16:18). The church belongs to Jesus—not the pastors, elders, deacons, or members. The Lord Jesus Christ is building the church. Nothing can defeat the church of Christ.

Christ is the head of the church. And Christ does not have out-of-body experiences. To submit to the authority of Jesus Christ over your life is to live in fellowship with the church.

Why the church?

FAITH IN GOD IS PRACTICED IN COMMUNITY

The unbelieving society we live in claims that faith is a private matter. Fact-check: Wrong! Indeed, faith is a personal matter. As Jesus told Nicodemus, "You must be born again" (John 3:7). But personal faith is not private faith. Faith in God is to be lived in fellowship with other believers. In the Old Testament, the faith community was the nation of Israel. In the New Testament, it is the church, a new community in Christ that transcends gender, race, or status (Gal. 3:28). To follow the Lord Jesus is to join the company of His disciples (Matt. 28:18–20).

THE CHURCH IS THE HOUSEHOLD OF GOD

Writing to Timothy in Ephesus, Paul called the church "the household of God, which is the church of the living God, a pillar and buttress of the truth" (1 Tim. 3:15). In salvation, we are born again and adopted into the family of God. A newborn child needs to become part of a household for nourishment, fellowship, and protection. The church is the household of faith (Gal. 6:10). More than that, it is God's household. To reject the church is to reject the means of care the Lord has provided for His redeemed children. The local church is the spiritual household where our heavenly Father nurtures His adopted children to maturity in Christ.

CHURCH MEMBERSHIP BRINGS
ASSURANCE OF SALVATION

A Christian is one who has professed saving faith in the Lord Jesus Christ. And that personal profession is best made to and among the church for there to be genuine discipleship. In the New Testament letters, the two essential marks of true conversion are faith in the Lord Jesus Christ and love for all the saints (Eph. 1:15; Col. 1:4). Christian fellowship is as essential to the authenticity of salvation as personal faith. Love for the saints demonstrates faith in Christ. "We know that we have passed out of death into life, because we love the brothers," wrote the apostle John. "Whoever does not love abides in death" (1 John 3:14).

THE CHURCH IS SPIRITUALLY UNITED TO CHRIST

In the Gospels, Jesus called would-be disciples to follow Him. But the actual relationship between Christ and His followers goes beyond that: "Christ in you, the hope of glory" (Col. 1:27). No other religion speaks of the relationship between its leader and adherents that way. This is the spiritual union between Christ and the church. As the fish is in the water and the water is in the fish, we are in Christ, and Christ is in us. As the bird is in the air and the air is in the bird, we are in Christ, and Christ is in us. This spiritual union with Christ is what binds us together as the church. The indwelling presence of the Life-Giver King resides within each of us and has made us one in Christ.

THE LORD JESUS CHRIST IS THE HEAD OF THE CHURCH

The church is often spurned because of things members of the church do or do not do. But no leader or member of the church is the standard by which we measure what the church should be.

Christ is the standard. He is the head of the church. The church is the body of Christ. The church is safe and secure in Him, as you cannot drown with your head above water. "The church is full of hypocrites," it is complained. But Christ is no hypocrite! He is the Truth (John 14:6). If Christ is not a hypocrite, He is worthy of our trust and obedience, even if He tells us to hang out with a bunch of hypocrites!

THE CHURCH IS THE MOST VALUABLE THING ON EARTH

Paul advised the Ephesian elders, "Pay careful attention to yourselves and to all the flock, in which the Holy Spirit has made you overseers, to care for the church of God, which he obtained with his own blood" (Acts 20:28). Think about the magnitude of this statement. God the Father purchased the church by the atoning blood of the Lord Jesus Christ. There is no institution in the world more valuable than that—not family, not business, not the government. Many worthy causes in the world deserve our support. But no worldly cause should usurp our commitment to the church for which Christ died. The church is the hope of the world.

> **Many worthy causes in the world deserve our support. But no worldly cause should usurp our commitment to the church for which Christ died.**

THE CHURCH IS THE OUTWORKING OF GOD'S ETERNAL PURPOSE

Holy Scripture is not a haphazard collection of stories, poetry, and letters. It is the unfolding of a divine plan. God initiated His plan of redemption in eternity past. It will be fully accomplished in eternity future. The church is essential to the eternal purpose of

God. Paul declared "the plan of the mystery hidden for ages in God, who created all things, so that through the church the manifold wisdom of God might be made known to the rulers and authorities in the heavenly places" (Eph. 3:9–10). The church is not incidental to the plan of God. It is the platform of the glory of God in the heavenly places. Our salvation in Christ is so glorious that the angels long to understand the grace of God to us (1 Peter 1:12).

THE CHURCH IS AN EARTHLY EXPRESSION OF HEAVEN

What do you think heaven is like? To answer that question, turn to Scripture, not near-death fantasies. For all we do not know about heaven, Scripture makes it clear that heaven will be filled with the glory of God. In this regard, the church is to be a reflection of heaven on earth. Church growth experts often advise pastors to shape the church around the desires, opinions, and values of the culture. But a "user-friendly" philosophy of ministry only makes the church like the world. The church should be shaped around the character of God. Only the church can display the truth, love, and holiness of God, as it is in heaven.

YOUR SANCTIFICATION IS A COMMUNITY PROJECT

Hebrews counsels, "And let us consider how to stir up one another to love and good works, not neglecting to meet together, as is the habit of some, but encouraging one another, and all the more as you see the Day drawing near" (Heb. 10:24–25). This is why we must not neglect to meet together with the church for corporate and public worship. Many Christians feel it is no big deal if they miss a Sunday or two. However, Scripture teaches, "But exhort one another every day, as long as it is called 'today,' that none of you may be hardened by the deceitfulness of sin" (Heb. 3:13). We are so weak, sin is so great, and the world is so evil; we need to be exhorted to live for Christ daily. We cannot afford to miss the meeting of God's people. We need God's people to stir us up to love God and serve others.

Vada May was a member of my father's congregation. I also had the privilege of being her pastor in her later years, as her health declined. Even then she did not miss a meeting if she could help it. She was too weak to actively serve. But her faithful presence was a great encouragement to the entire congregation. How much more should this be the case with those of us who have the health, strength, and opportunity to meet together to build up one another.

Chapter 7

WORSHIP AND DISCIPLE-MAKING

Matthew 28:18–20 states the mission of the church: "All authority in heaven and on earth has been given to me. Go therefore and make disciples of all nations, baptizing them in the name of the Father and of the Son and of the Holy Spirit, teaching them to observe all that I have commanded you. And behold, I am with you always, to the end of the age."

By the time you get to this final passage in Matthew's gospel, the death, burial, and resurrection of Jesus have already taken place. All that is left for Matthew to report is the promised post-resurrection meetings of Jesus and His disciples: "Now the eleven disciples went to Galilee, to the mountain to which Jesus had directed them. And when they saw him they worshiped him, but some doubted" (vv. 16–17). After this summary, Matthew tells us that Jesus came to the disciples and gave the Great Commission.

Feel the tension between the setting of the Great Commission (vv. 16–17) and the statement of the Great Commission (vv. 18–20).

The disciples trekked up some unidentified but predetermined Galilean mountainside to meet their risen Savior. (It was now eleven of them as the betrayer, Judas, had committed suicide.) They arrived first and awaited Jesus' arrival. Then they saw a man approaching from a distance. When the disciples caught a good glimpse of Jesus walking toward them, they fell on their faces. With their faces on the ground, they worshiped. Yet, notes Matthew, as they worshiped, some of them did not really believe it was Jesus.

In the upper room, Phillip had asked Jesus to show them the Father (John 14:8). Jerome Kirby called this "an elementary question on graduation day." Jesus rebuked him for not knowing that anyone who had seen Him had seen the Father (John 14:9). You would think Jesus would rebuke these "worshiping" disciples who did not recognize Him. But that is not what happened. Jesus proceeded to entrust His world mission to these very men.

Think about that. The Lord chose limited, fallible, and sinful human beings as His vehicle to spread the most important message of all. He could have chosen angels to do the job. He could have parted the clouds and spoken audibly to lost humanity. As in days past, He could have spoken through a burning bush, appeared in a vision, or carved His message on stone tablets. Instead, the Lord chose ordinary people to carry His message of salvation to the nations.

THE POWER AND AUTHORITY OF THE MISSION

The early church carried out the mission and message of Christ with boldness, power, and fruitfulness. When Paul and Silas arrived in Thessalonica, the unbelieving people declared, "These men who have turned the world upside down have come here also" (Acts 17:6). I believe the gospel of Jesus Christ still has the power to turn the world upside down. Do you? How, then, did the Great Commission become the great omission? It is because we try to fulfill the mission of Jesus without acknowledging the authority of Jesus.

The Great Commission begins with a bold declaration of sovereign authority: "All authority in heaven and on earth has been given to me" (Matt. 28:18). This is one of the most important Christological statements in the New Testament. It is a claim, not a commission. But the commission rests on this claim. If verse 18 is not true, verses 19–20 are meaningless.

Jesus claims power of attorney to exercise divine sovereignty. The scope of Christ's authority is stated in one word: "all." It is tempting to begin listing the earthly powers over which Jesus exercises authority. But suffice it to say that if Jesus has all authority, all other authorities are subject to the lordship of Christ. The sphere of Jesus' authority is "in heaven and on earth."

Jesus reigns over all the spirit beings in the heavens—holy and fallen. And Jesus reigns over all human beings on the earth, regardless of race, culture, background, status, or any other factor. Abraham Kuyper rightly said "there is not a square inch in the whole domain of our human existence over which Christ, who is Sovereign over *all*, does not cry: 'Mine!'"[4]

Do not judge the authority of Jesus by the breaking news of the day. The proof of Christ's authority is that He lived to make this claim. Jesus was betrayed, arrested, tried, convicted, sentenced, beaten, and crucified. But God raised Him from the dead and gave Him all authority over heaven and earth.

This great claim is a declaration of war against the enemies of God (Acts 17:30–31). It is also the basis of the marching orders of the church (Matt. 28:19–20). The church exists to make more and better disciples of the Lord Jesus Christ. This mission is as small as the neighbors on your block and as large as the almost eight billion people in the world.

We are to make disciples through personal evangelism.

We are to mark disciples through water baptism.

We are to mature disciples through biblical teaching.

The Great Commission entrusts one singular, primary, and definitive function to the church—to make disciples of Jesus. The church is not a social club, political action committee, or civil rights organization. The church is the assembly of redeemed disciples who reproduce themselves life on life. But you do not get a church to execute the mission by emphasizing the mission. On-mission churches are Christ-exalting churches. John Piper said it best: "Missions is not the ultimate goal of the church. Worship is. Missions exists because worship doesn't."[5]

> **The church is not a social club, political action committee, or civil rights organization. The church is the assembly of redeemed disciples who reproduce themselves life on life.**

Worship is not merely one of many good things the church does. It is the heart of what the church is and does. Worship must be the heart of the church because Christ is the head of the church. He is our all-sufficient Prophet, Priest, and King. Paul wrote, "And he is the head of the body, the church. He is the beginning, the firstborn from the dead, that in everything he might be preeminent" (Col. 1:18). Worshiping the sovereign majesty of Christ fuels the church to pursue our mission freely, faithfully, and fruitfully.

TO ALL THE NATIONS

The church began in Jerusalem with Jewish converts. But it was not to stay that way (Acts 1:8). Through a dramatic vision, the Lord confronted and corrected Peter's view of Gentiles (Acts 10:9–33). In the aftermath, Peter declared, "Truly I understand that God shows no partiality, but in every nation anyone who fears him and does what is right is acceptable to him" (Acts 10:34–35).

It was not the power of the vision that changed Peter's mind. It was the authority of Christ. When the authority of Christ is not exalted, our gospel mission is short-circuited. We will make disciples of our "tribe" rather than all the nations. The call to make disciples requires that we meet weekly to be reminded in worship that the risen Christ rules and reigns.

The church cannot succeed if it depends on any other authority but Christ. God's work cannot be advanced in human strength. Therefore, we must not trust gimmicks, programs, events, traditions, or personalities. The church's mission is accomplished by the authority of Christ alone (John 15:5; 2 Cor. 3:5). In addition, the church cannot succeed by doing things that Christ has not authorized. He only blesses what is His. Let me bottom-line that for you.

We must not preach a message that Christ has not authorized.

We must not follow leaders whom Christ has not authorized.

We must not commit to goals that Christ has not authorized.

We must not engage in practices that Christ has not authorized.

We must not go in any direction that Christ has not authorized.

Only by the authority of Christ can we make disciples locally and globally with His assurance, "Behold, I am with you always, to the end of the age" (Matt. 28:20b).

✝

Chapter 8

TOTAL-LIFE STEWARDSHIP

What does stewardship have to do with worship? Everything. Stewardship is essential to worship. One cannot exist without the other.

In the Old Testament, the most basic act of worship—presenting an offering to be sacrificed to God on the altar—was about what people gave to God, not the other way around. Every Old Testament act of worship, personal or corporate, was Godward, not manward. The nature of worship does not change in the New Testament. But our focus of worship has shifted. We rate the service by how much we get out of it. We have forgotten that worship is more about what you offer to God than what you receive from God. Stewardship is worship.

In the church I grew up in, stewardship was defined narrowly—giving your time, talents, and treasures. These three aspects of stewardship are the truth, but not the whole truth. Stewardship is more than how you spend your money, manage your schedule, and use your gifts. It is total-life stewardship. All of life is a sacred trust for which you must give an account to God.

The bottom line of Christian stewardship can be stated in four words: God owns it all. David audited God's assets and reported

God's portfolio: "The earth is the LORD's and the fullness thereof, the world and those who dwell therein" (Ps. 24:1).

Everything we possess belongs to God. We have one duty to the God who has richly given us all things to enjoy: "Moreover, it is required of stewards that they be found faithful" (1 Cor. 4:2). Why should we live faithfully? Paul answers, "For we must all appear before the judgment seat of Christ, so that each one may receive what is due for what he has done in the body, whether good or evil" (2 Cor. 5:10).

Stewardship is about much more than financial offerings. It involves every facet of life. Romans 12:1 says, "I appeal to you therefore, brothers, by the mercies of God, to present your bodies as a living sacrifice, holy and acceptable to God, which is your spiritual worship." This call to worship involves more than Sunday service. It calls for devotion to the Lord on a day-to-day basis. It is life worship, not just lip worship. What does it mean to worship God with your life?

THE STEWARDSHIP OF YOUR TIME

Time is life. We live our lives confined to the passing moments of our brief time on this earth. That time passes fast. It is vital that we make the most of every opportunity. This doesn't happen through time-management techniques or time-saving technologies. It only happens by a high view of God. Isn't it interesting that Jesus was never in a hurry, but He always had the time to do God's will? We are always in a hurry and rarely have time to do God's will. We worship God by being good stewards of the time He has given us. Pray with Moses: "So teach us to number our days that we may get a heart of wisdom" (Ps. 90:12).

THE STEWARDSHIP OF YOUR RELATIONSHIPS

Did you know your relationships are a gift from God? I know it may not seem that way with some people you have to deal with. It's true, nonetheless. Difficult people are providentially placed in your life for your sanctification. The fruit of the Spirit (Gal. 5:22–23) is cultivated in the soil of relationships. Messy relationships. You are not responsible for how people treat you. But you are responsible for your role in your relationships. To be a faithful steward of your relationships, focus on your character and the other person's needs, not vice versa.

THE STEWARDSHIP OF YOUR FINANCES

Many people think their problems would be solved if they had more money. They fail to realize the critical issue is rarely how much they have, but what they do with what they have. We worship God by being faithful with the money He entrusts to us. Jesus said,

> "One who is faithful in a very little is also faithful in much, and the one who is dishonest in a very little is also dishonest in much. If then you have not been faithful in the unrighteous wealth, who will entrust to you the true riches? And if you have not been faithful in that which is another's, who will give you that which is your own? No servant can serve two masters, for either he will hate the one and love the other, or he will be devoted to the one and despise the other. You cannot serve God and money." (Luke 16:10–13)

THE STEWARDSHIP OF YOUR BODY

Paul asked the Corinthians, "Or do you not know that your body is a temple of the Holy Spirit within you, whom you have from

God? You are not your own, for you were bought with a price. So glorify God in your body" (1 Cor. 6:19–20). Strive to be healthy. This involves treating your body as a temple in which God dwells, not sacrificing your body on the altar of society's idolatrous fixation with physical fitness, sex appeal, and cosmetic beauty. Christian diets, workout regimes, and fashion tips are not what the stewardship of the body is about, though stewardship does include proper care of our bodies. Strive for holiness. Paul advised Timothy to "train yourself for godliness; for while bodily training is of some value, godliness is of value in every way, as it holds promise for the present life and also for the life to come" (1 Tim. 4:7b–8).

THE STEWARDSHIP OF YOUR SPEECH

Words are powerful. They are like nitroglycerin: they can either blow up bridges or heal hearts. No wonder God places such a premium on the words we speak. God is listening to the words we say. And that is not limited to the words of praise we sing in church. In everything we say, our words are either offerings of worship or tools of the enemy. Solomon warned, "When words are many, transgression is not lacking, but whoever restrains his lips is prudent" (Prov. 10:19). Jesus said, "I tell you, on the day of judgment people will give account for every careless word they speak" (Matt. 12:36). And Paul admonished, "Let no corrupting talk come out of your mouths, but only such as is good for building up, as fits the occasion, that it may give grace to those who hear" (Eph. 4:29).

THE STEWARDSHIP OF YOUR GIFTS

Spiritual gifts are a confusing and controversial subject. But the New Testament is clear about two principles: (1) every Christian has received at least one spiritual gift, and (2) we are accountable to

God for the proper use of those gifts. Peter instructs, "As each has received a gift, use it to serve one another, as good stewards of God's varied grace" (1 Peter 4:10). The New Testament does not tell us how to discover our spiritual gifts. It emphasizes all Christians are gifted and orders us to use our gifts for the good of others and the glory of God.

Christian service is essential to our understanding of Christian worship. When we worship corporately, we do not gather to be served by others. God has gifted us to serve others and will hold us accountable for the stewardship of our gifts.

THE STEWARDSHIP OF YOUR WITNESS

After His resurrection and before His ascension, Jesus said to the disciples, "But you will receive power when the Holy Spirit has come upon you, and you will be my witnesses in Jerusalem and in all Judea and Samaria, and to the end of the earth" (Acts 1:8). The word *witness* translated the term from which we get our English word *martyr*. We typically think of martyrdom in reference to those who die for their witness for Christ. In the New Testament, the term also refers to living witnesses. Paul writes, "This is how one should regard us, as servants of Christ and stewards of the mysteries of God" (1 Cor. 4:1). This is not just the task of New Testament apostles. It is the task of all Christians.

Christ has called us to be the salt of the earth and the light of the world (Matt. 5:13–16). Our worship and our witness go together. Live, serve, and witness in unwavering faithfulness to hear the Master say, "Well done, good and faithful servant" at the final inspection (Matt. 25:23).

Chapter 9

BIBLICAL REASONS FOR GENEROUS GIVING

Giving is a part of worship."

I regularly heard this statement in church as a youth. As the congregation walked around the collection plate, they would start greeting one another and talking to friends. The offering would sometimes feel like recess at school. When the noise level became a little too high, the preacher warned the church that we were still in worship, even though it was the offering.

The preacher was right. Giving is a part of worship. It is a key part of worship, not a functional add-on to receive donations. Moreover, giving *is* worship. It is a fundamental element of worship. It is essential to what worship is all about. The heart of all of our worship is about what we give to God.

Too many of us have the give-and-receive positions in worship mixed up. We think of worship in terms of what we receive from God. Or we think Sunday worship is a time to say thanks for what we have received in anticipation of what we will receive in the days to come. The self-centered mindset disregards the God-centered nature of worship.

The true worshiper gives himself to the Lord, first and foremost. With a life devoted to the Lord, we offer our possessions to acknowledge His authority over our lives, give thanks for His undeserved goodness to us, and invest in the kingdom of heaven. There are four fundamental reasons that you should give to God regularly, generously, and sacrificially.

GOD OWNS WHAT I POSSESS

The first step toward becoming more generous requires that you and I acknowledge that what we give to God already belongs to God. We give back to a giving God, who still owns what He gives.

The bottom line of Christian stewardship can be stated in four words: God owns it all.

"But who am I, and what is my people, that we should be able thus to offer willingly?" David prayed. "For all things come from you, and of your own have we given you" (1 Chron. 29:14). In a real sense, we never really give anything to God. Whatever we give to the Lord already belongs to Him. It is like a child buying his father a birthday present with his father's money. The son may give his dad a gift from his heart, but it is not from his resources.

The bottom line of Christian stewardship can be stated in four words: God owns it all. David audited the Lord's resources and reported a statement of his divine assets: "The earth is the LORD's and the fullness thereof, the world and those who dwell therein, for he has founded it upon the seas and established it upon the rivers" (Ps. 24:1–2).

We own nothing. God owns everything. We are just stewards, managers of the material possessions God entrusts to us. A steward must be faithful to the one who owns what he manages. Jesus said,

"One who is faithful in a very little is also faithful in much, and one who is dishonest in a very little is also dishonest in much. If then you have not been faithful in the unrighteous wealth, who will entrust to you the true riches? And if you have not been faithful in that which is another's, who will give you that which is your own?" (Luke 16:10–12)

GOD MULTIPLIES WHAT I GIVE

"What difference does my giving make?" We may be tempted to ask that when we consider our small resources and the needs of our church, community, and city—not to mention the larger world around us. It's a natural question. But to ask it is to have the wrong focus in giving. The bottom line is that your offering to God is never too small.

When the lad's lunch was presented to Jesus to feed the crowd, Andrew asked, "But what are they for so many?" (John 6:9). Sometimes we feel that way. Our gift is so small. The needs are so great. What difference will my gift make? The answer: little becomes much when you place it in the Master's hands. Jesus sees the widow's mite (Mark 12:41–44). God counts our offering by the attitude of our heart, not the amount in our hand. Paul wrote, "For if the readiness is there, it is acceptable according to what a person has, not according to what he does not have" (2 Cor. 8:12).

Likewise, your offering to God is never too big. You can never give too much to God! Your attitude toward giving should not be, "What's the least I can give?" Rather, you should sing with the psalmist, "What shall I render to the LORD for all his benefits to me?" (Ps. 116:12). Mark it down: you cannot beat God in giving! "Give and it shall be given to you," Jesus promised. "Good measure pressed down, shaken together, running over, will be put into your lap" (Luke 6:38).

GOD REWARDS WHAT I INVEST

There is a difference between an expense and an investment. An expense comes out of your account. Period. An investment comes out of your account with the expectation that it will bring a return at some point in the future.

When you give to God, it is always an investment. It is an investment with guaranteed rewards. "Do not lay up for yourselves treasures on earth, where moth and rust destroy and where thieves break in and steal, but lay up for yourselves treasures in heaven, where neither moth nor rust destroys and where thieves do not break in and steal. For where your treasure is, there your heart will be also" (Matt. 6:19–21). This is the treasure principle: you cannot take it with you. But you can send it on ahead of you!

Therefore, invest in the poor: "Whoever is generous to the poor lends to the LORD, and he will repay him for his deed" (Prov. 19:17). Invest in the next generation: "A good man leaves an inheritance to his children's children, but the sinner's wealth is laid up for the righteous" (Prov. 13:22).

Most importantly, invest in the church: "The point is this: whoever sows sparingly will also reap sparingly, and whoever sows bountifully will also reap bountifully. Each one must give as he has decided in his heart, not reluctantly or under compulsion, for God loves a cheerful giver" (2 Cor. 9:6–7). The church is the hope of the world. We have the only message that can save lost people. When you invest in the church to advance the truth, hope, and love of Christ to the world, God will not allow your investment to go unrewarded!

GOD SUPPLIES WHAT I NEED

If I give generously, how will I take care of my own needs? What about my bills, goals, and responsibilities? How will I face whatever tomorrow brings? These worries prevent many from giving to the work of Christ. But the Word of God directly addresses these concerns.

God issues the command to give with a promise of blessing: "Bring the full tithe into the storehouse, that there may be food in my house. And thereby put me to the test, says the LORD of hosts, if I will not open the windows of heaven for you and pour down for you a blessing until there is no more need" (Mal. 3:10). Typically, God warns man not to put Him to the test. When it comes to giving, God invites it. God puts His reputation on the line that He will provide for those who give generously.

The promise of Philippians 4:19 is for all who sacrifice for the work of God: "And my God will supply every need of yours according to his riches in glory in Christ Jesus." This is the cashier's check the generous Christian carries in the wallet of faith. There is the sovereign Banker: "my God." There is the insurance policy: "shall supply." There is the check amount: "every need of yours." There is the account balance: "according to his riches in glory." There is the check signatory: "in Christ Jesus."

Chapter 10

✝

THE TEST OF TRUE WORSHIP

Job was a rich man and a righteous man (Job 1:1–5). Satan claimed Job was only righteous because he was rich. The devil accused God of bribing Job with blessings. He also accused Job of only serving God for the benefits he received. If the favorable circumstances changed, Satan assured God, Job would curse God to His face.

The Lord accepted Satan's challenge. As a result, Job was caught in the crossfire of a cosmic bet. The Lord lifted His hedge of protection from Job's life. And Satan attacked. One day, Job was ambushed by the unexpected. He received bad news after bad news (Job 1:13–19). By the end of the day, Job lost everything. All of his possessions were stolen. All of his servants were murdered. All of his children died in a freak storm.

You misunderstand the story of Job if all you see in the story of Job is the story of Job. This story is not merely about Job. It is about you and me. If you have saving faith in the Lord Jesus Christ, the same satanic accusation against Job is being made against you.

Do you serve the Lord for His name's sake?

Or do you only serve the Lord to receive blessings?

This is the test of true worship. It is one thing to worship God when the sun is shining. It is another thing to worship God when the storm is raging. True worship is not fair-weather worship. True worship continues to worship God when the storms of life are raging. At some point, your worship of God will be tested by the trials of life.

Will you pass the test?

TRUE WORSHIP IS A CHOICE

Job 1:20 reports Job's natural reaction and spiritual response to the tragic news, unspeakable loss, and broken heart: "Then Job arose and tore his robe and shaved his head and fell on the ground and worshiped."

Tearing his robe and shaving his head were customary expressions of pain, grief, and sorrow. These were no mere ceremonial acts. Job grieved. Job exemplifies that there is nothing spiritual about acting like life does not hurt when life hurts. Being born again does not make you bionic. Godly people grieve. In Scripture, many godly people, including Abraham, Joseph, Moses, David, Jeremiah, Peter, and Paul, wept and mourned. Even Jesus wept at the graveside of Lazarus (John 11:35). The Bible does not forbid mourning. It admonishes us not to sorrow as those who have no hope (1 Thess. 4:13).

After Job tore his robe and shaved his head, he bowed to the ground. And with his face in the dirt, Job worshiped God. It is understandable that Job grieved his loss. It is what you would have done. But can you worship God with a broken heart? Job's godly response teaches us that worship is a choice. Believers suffer bad things in life, just like unbelievers. We grieve. They grieve. But we do not curse God, sin with our lips, or charge God with wrong.

God does not change when circumstances change. So we continue to worship God in sickness, sorrow, and suffering. The Bible teaches three facts of life:

God is good.

God is all-powerful.

Terrible things happen.

Any two of these facts make sense together, if you exclude one. To embrace all three makes no sense. Faith involves believing all three truths. The evidence of faith is that you continue to worship God, even when terrible things happen. Life is hard. But life is not God. God is God. And God is good all the time!

TRUE WORSHIP IS THE RESULT OF AN ETERNAL PERSPECTIVE

As Job worshiped, the media showed up. "Job, you've lost everything," a reporter said. "How do you feel?"

Job answered, "Naked I came from my mother's womb, and naked shall I return. The LORD gave, and the LORD has taken away; blessed be the name of the LORD" (Job 1:21). Job's eternal perspective was expressed in two statements about himself and three statements about the Lord.

Job made two statements about himself. First, he said, "Naked I came from my mother's womb." Job did not enter the world with cattle, money, servants, property, or children. Everything he possessed, he received. He came into the world naked. Everything he owned was a grace gift from God. Then Job said, "And naked shall I return." We checked into this world with nothing. We will check out with what we checked in with. We brought nothing into this world. And we will take nothing with us. A baby is born with a closed fist; a man dies with open hands. Death snatches away the material possessions we accumulate.

Job made three statements about the Lord. First, Job said, "The LORD gave." God is a generous God. Has not the Lord been good to you? Do not judge God's generosity by what is in your bank account. Divine generosity is ultimately demonstrated at the cross of the Lord Jesus Christ (John 3:16; 1 John 4:8–9).

Then Job said, "And the LORD has taken away." Job did not say the Lord gave, but Satan took away. God provided and withdrew Job's blessings. Good parents give both allowances and punishment to teach their children responsibility. So does God the Father. Finally, Job said, "Blessed be the name of the LORD." It is easy to say the Lord gave. It is hard to say the Lord has taken away. It is impossible to say blessed be the name of the Lord without an eternal perspective.

Job blessed the Lord because the Lord gives before He takes away.

Job blessed the Lord because the Lord gives more than He takes away.

Job blessed the Lord because He leaves us enough to make it even when the Lord takes away.

TRUE WORSHIP REQUIRES STUBBORN TRUST

Prosperity preachers claim Job made his situation worse by speaking a negative confession. God only gives and never takes away, they insist. This is further proof that the "money-cometh" hustlers only read the parts of the Bible that support their predetermined conclusions. Job 1:22 states: "In all this Job did not sin or charge God with wrong." Job's worship did not prevent Job from having to bury his ten children. Yet Job did not wrongly indict the goodness, wisdom, and sovereignty of God. Job trusted God's character even when God's ways did not make sense.

This is not the end of the story.

Job did not curse God. But Satan did not concede. He concluded that he did not hit Job hard enough. Satan asked permission to attack Job again. The Lord gave Satan free access to Job's life, only stipulating that the devil spare his life. This time, Satan attacked Job's health. "Do you still hold fast your integrity?" Job's wife asked her pain-stricken husband. "Curse God and die" (Job 2:9). Job's wife wrongly concluded that Job offended God. She advised Job to go all the way so God would strike him down. Job's wife was the ancient prototype of Dr. Kevorkian. She proposed the first "mercy-killing" to end her husband's misery.

Genuine faith is ambidextrous. It takes blessings in one hand and trouble in the other with stubborn trust, complete obedience, and unceasing praise.

"You speak as one of the foolish women would speak," Job responded. "Shall we receive good from God, and shall we not receive evil?" Again, Job did not sin with his lips (Job 2:10). It is not wrong to say the Lord gave and the Lord has taken away. It is wrong to receive blessings and refuse to receive trouble. There is a place where the sun always shines and it never rains. It's called a desert. Nothing grows in a desert, including faith in God. Genuine faith is ambidextrous. It takes blessings in one hand and trouble in the other with stubborn trust, complete obedience, and unceasing praise.

Part 2:

PARTICIPATING IN WORSHIP

Chapter 11

✝

ASSEMBLY REQUIRED

A friend and I had a long conversation, a typical discussion that happens when pastors get together. We fixed all of the problems in the church and the world before we got up from the table. Of course, nothing changed when we finished our profound conversation.

After an extended debate about transitions and succession, we considered our future retirements from pastoral ministry, God willing. "When I retire, I'm not going to church anymore," my friend joked. "I will do like my members and just watch the services via livestream." My friend assured me that he would faithfully pay his tithes and offerings each week. But he would do so from the comfort of his fishing boat on Sunday mornings. We laughed heartily. Then the conversation moved on to other topics. But the question my friend raised kept gnawing at me.

Would you go to church if you were not a pastor?

There are times I feel like the man who slept in one Sunday morning. His wife insisted he get ready for church. "Give me three reasons why I should go to church today," he mumbled.

His wife had three ready answers. "First, it's Sunday, and it is your Christian duty to worship. Second, the Lord has been good, and we should give thanks for His blessings. Third, you're the pastor of the church!"

Yes, I am a pastor who is paid to be at church on Sundays. It is my responsibility to be present and prepared to serve each week. I take these duties seriously. Pastoral ministry has been a vital part of the Lord's sanctifying work in my life. But I do not go to church merely because I am a pastor who must be there. I would go to church even if I were not a pastor.

I would go to church if I were not a pastor because I would still be a Christian if I were not a pastor. To be a Christian is to be a participating member of the local church. There are many reasons professing Christians stop going to church. Few acknowledge John's explanation: "They went out from us, but they were not of us; for if they had been of us, they would have continued with us. But they went out, that it might become plain that they all are not of us" (1 John 2:19).

Church hurt is a real thing. But the Lord has given instructions for dealing with unrepentant sinners in the church (Matt. 18:15–20). The Lord's solution is church discipline, not church abandonment. If you are part of a church that refuses to practice church discipline, that is a different matter. Find a church that faithfully submits to the commands of Christ. Christ promises to be with the two or three gathered in His name to preserve fidelity of doctrine, holiness of life, and unity of fellowship in the church.

"The church is full of hypocrites," some claim. I could not disagree more. Most importantly, the Lord Jesus Christ is not a hypocrite. He is the Way, the Truth, and the Life (John 14:6). The Lord is worthy of our trust, obedience, and worship, even if He commands me to join a bunch of hypocrites!

There are many good reasons that I would go to church if I were not a preacher. The primary reason is that Christ is the head of the church, and the church is the body of Christ. You cannot have a high view of Christ and a low view of the church.

I love Jesus Christ. And I love what Jesus loves. Christ loves the church and gave Himself for her (Eph. 5:25). Christ is sanctifying the church to present her to Himself without spot or blemish. In the meantime, "Let us consider how to stir up one another to love and good works, not neglecting to meet together, as is the habit of some, but encouraging one another, and all the more as you see the Day drawing near" (Heb. 10:24–25).

Here are twenty-five reasons you should regularly participate in public and corporate worship:

1. The Word of God teaches it (Heb. 10:24–25). A high and correct view of Scripture demands regular church attendance.

2. Corporate worship is where the preaching and teaching of God's Word occur (2 Tim. 4:1–5).

3. It follows the example set by the Lord Jesus Christ (Luke 4:16).

4. It honors the best and brightest day of the week—Sunday, the Lord's Day—the day on which the Lord Jesus rose from the dead.

5. It is a wise and proper use of the privilege we have to publicly and corporately worship God. Christians in other lands do not all have this freedom. The only way for us to express our gratitude for this liberty is to use it faithfully and thankfully.

6. Your neglect of corporate worship grieves the Holy Spirit who lives within the individual believer and the church as a whole (Eph. 4:30).

7. It brings joy to the spiritual leaders who watch over your soul and who must give account for you. Absenteeism grieves them and is unprofitable for you (Heb. 13:17).

8. It demonstrates that you share the mission and ministry of the particular church family of which you are a member.

9. Your absence from church services renders it difficult, and in some instances impossible, for you to participate in the church's mutual ministry to itself, especially the "one an-other" commands of the New Testament.

10. You need the encouragement that comes from the assem-bling of the saints (Heb. 10:24–25). The more evil the days become, the more you need this encouragement.

11. God demands first place (Matt. 6:33). This principle should govern our practice.

12. It reminds you that God has a new community of people through faith in Jesus Christ (Rom. 12:5).

13. It is a way of preserving the unity of the Spirit in the bond of peace (Eph. 4:3).

14. Public and corporate worship is the central place where you exercise your spiritual gifts. It is a strategic place to minister to other believers (1 Cor. 14:12).

15. Your regular attendance serves as a positive example and influence for others.

16. If you participate in some ministry of the church—and you should—your absence can hinder the overall effectiveness of the group and discourage other members.

17. Being involved in public and corporate worship services counteracts our self-centeredness.

18. You should take the time to stop and say "thank You" to God for bringing you through another week.

19. Absenteeism is a poor testimony to unbelievers who see your inconsistency (John 13:34–35). It is also a poor witness to our children, whom we are to raise in the instruction and admonition of the Lord.

20. True and saving faith will foster love for that which Christ loves, the church (Eph. 5:25). Regularly attending church services is a fundamental way to demonstrate your love for the bride of Christ.

21. The practice of good habits like regular church attendance builds spiritual character.

22. The New Testament teaches us to recognize, share all good things with, submit to, and honor spiritual leaders who teach us the Word. Attending worship is a way of doing that. (Remember, not only are we accountable to the Word of God, but we are also accountable to those whom God uses to teach us His Word.)

23. Attending public and corporate worship services renews and strengthens us for the days ahead (Heb. 10:24–25).

24. Corporate worship helps reinforce the truth that worship is not about getting from God. Fundamentally, Christian worship is about giving to God.

25. Public and corporate worship is the officially designated place to carry out the ordinances of the church—baptism and the Lord's Supper.

Chapter 12

✝

PRAYING FOR SUNDAY

Corporate worship is spiritual warfare. Every time the redeemed community of the baptized in Christ meets for worship, Satan fights back. Warren W. Wiersbe wrote: "God and Satan have this in common: each desires our worship. God wants us to worship Him because He is worthy, and He graciously wants to transform us. Satan wants our worship because he wants to destroy us, and worship is the easiest way to achieve that diabolical purpose."[6]

As we gather to offer praise, we must be strong in the Lord and the power of His might (Eph. 6:10). We have the whole armor of God to enable us to stand firm against the schemes of the devil (Eph. 6:11–13). Paul listed the armor God has given us in Ephesians 6:14–17. In verses 18–20, the military metaphor is dropped, but the subject of warfare continues. Paul calls for warfare prayer.

I call prayer the believer's secret weapon. The armor listed in verses 14–17 corresponds with the Roman soldier's battle gear. But the Roman soldier did not have anything to compare to what the believer has in prayer. In the heat of the battle, a centurion could not call on Caesar for help. But the child of God may call on God for help and strength in prayer. The enemy and his forces conflict with the worshiping people of God. We must cover our worship services in believing prayer.

As He cleansed the temple of the money changers and dove sellers, Jesus declared, "It is written, 'My house shall be called a house of prayer,' but you make it a den of robbers" (Matt. 21:13). Confirming the Word of God in the Old Testament (Isa. 56:7; Jer. 7:11), Jesus asserted that the temple was to be a house of prayer for all nations.

Throughout this book, we have talked much about music, preaching, and other elements of corporate worship. But Jesus did not say the temple was to be a house of preaching or singing. It was to be a house of prayer. In the New Testament, we are the temple, and as we gather to worship or worship privately, prayer fuels worship. Everything we understand in the name of the Lord should be seasoned and marinated in prayer.

Being a house of prayer does not mean that there should be a prayer ministry in the church. It does not mean that there should be some saints in the church who are "prayer warriors." And it does not mean that there should be scheduled prayer meetings on the church's calendar. All of these things are great to have. But being a house of prayer involves much more. It is to be a house that is characterized by prayer.

A guest or new member should not have to look at a church's regular schedule or ministry program list to discover it is a house of prayer. Colossians 4:2 says, "Continue steadfastly in prayer, being watchful in it with thanksgiving." This duty involves our corporate worship services, as well as our private prayer closets. When the church meets for worship, our services should reflect our steadfast devotion to prayer. Our worship services should be prayer services.

POWERFUL PRAYER

Paul wrote, "First of all, then, I urge that supplications, prayers, intercessions, and thanksgivings be made for all people, for kings and all who are in high positions, that we may lead a peaceful and quiet life, godly and dignified in every way" (1 Tim. 2:1–2).

I cannot count how many times I have had a conference "stage manager" tell me that when the lead singer prays, that will be my sign to go to the podium. And when I finish the message, please close in prayer to give the music team time to get in place for the closing song. I can only hope this is not how prayer is treated (or mistreated) in our local churches on the Lord's Day. Prayer should not be a transitional element to maintain the pace and schedule of the service. Prayer should be central to everything that takes place in the worship service.

If you have a leadership role at church, pray to invoke God's presence and blessings. Offer prayers of praise and thanksgiving for the goodness of God to us in the Lord Jesus Christ. Make petitions of confession of sin and give assurance of forgiveness through the finished work of Christ. Lead pastoral payers for the work of the church, the spread of the gospel, and the needs of the congregation. Pray over the financial offerings that will be presented in worship to God. Pray before the sermon and after the sermon. Find any excuse in the service to advertise your dependence upon God in prayer.

Indeed, the church should pray on Sunday. The church should also pray for Sunday. You should participate in the prayer times of the worship services. Throughout the week, however, you should spend time in prayer for the upcoming worship services. Pray for the atmosphere of the service. Pray for the leaders of the service. Pray for the elements of the service. Pray for the participants of the service. Pray for the fruitfulness of the service.

PAUL'S PRAYER FOR THE SAINTS

Paul often prayed for the saints. Likewise, Paul often asked the saints to pray for him. In some instances, Paul wrote to people he led to Christ and churches he planted. Yet Paul solicited their prayers. Paul made some of these prayer requests from prison, yet he did not ask the saints to pray for his safety in prison or his release from prison.

Paul asked the church to pray "that words may be given to me in opening my mouth boldly to proclaim the mystery of the gospel, for which I am an ambassador in chains, that I may declare it boldly, as I ought to speak" (Eph. 6:19–20). These are vital requests to pray for your pastor as he prepares to preach the Word. Pray the Lord would give him the right words to say. Pray that God would grant him clarity of speech to make known the mystery of the gospel. Pray the Lord to grant him the courage to say what he ought to say.

Your pastor stands to preach each week. Some sermons are better than others, but if he is well-prepared each week, it is not just because your pastor is a good communicator. Sermons do not grow on trees! Biblical preaching is hard work. Sure, there are preachers who do it well and make it look so easy. In most instances, the good preachers work hard to make it look easy. Pray for your pastor's sermon preparation.

There are certain people I do not like to go out to eat with. They are the types who give the waiter or waitress a hard time, and I have a cardinal rule: do not cause trouble for the person who will bring me my food. This should be your attitude toward the pastor who feeds you the Word of God. Look out for your spiritual waiter by praying for his devotion to Christ, selection of texts, study of the passage, crafting of the message, and delivery of the sermon. Ask him how you can be praying for his sermon preparation and commit yourself to pray for him as he prepares.

It is said that the "power room" of Charles Spurgeon's Metropolitan Tabernacle in London was under the sanctuary where a group gathered to pray as he preached. Does your church have a power room? If not, work with your church leaders to establish one. Be your pastor's partner in prayer. Invite other members to join you in praying for Sunday. Pray that "God may open . . . a door for the word" (Col. 4:3) and that it would run swiftly to save the lost and sanctify the church to the glory of God.

Chapter 13

✝

SUNDAY MORNING BEGINS ON SATURDAY NIGHT

We've all done it. We have participated in worship services without worshiping God in spirit and truth. We have gone through the motions. We have sat in services with our minds and hearts in some faraway place.

Why does this happen? You love God. You are a devoted follower of the Lord Jesus Christ. You believe in the Holy Spirit. You are a participating member of your local church, and you looked forward to church all week. The worship was uplifting, the music was inspiring, and the sermon was edifying. But, somehow, you missed it all.

As the congregation offered worship, you were faultfinding.

As musical praise went forth, you thoughtlessly mouthed the words.

As the pastor preached the Word, you were daydreaming.

You know what it is to share Jacob's sad post-Bethel lament: "Surely the LORD is in this place, and I did not know it" (Gen. 28:16).

What happened? One of the reasons we "miss" some of the worship services we attend is that we start preparing for worship too late.

WHO PREPARES FOR WORSHIP?

Before I go any further, let me ask a direct question.

Do you prepare for worship? You expect the teaching pastor, music leaders, and ministry volunteers to prepare to lead. Do you prepare to participate? On Sunday mornings, do you get up, get dressed, and go to church without preparation? Or do you take great care to prepare yourself physically, making sure your attire and appearance are presentable—while your heart and mind are not? Do you prepare your inner person to gather with the redeemed saints before the throne of grace?

Solomon warned, "Guard your steps when you go to the house of God" (Eccl. 5:1). Do these words reflect how you approach your meeting place for corporate worship? Do you go to church carefully, thoughtfully, prayerfully? Can you sing with the Sons of Korah, "How lovely is your dwelling place, O Lord of hosts! My soul longs, yes, faints for the courts of the Lord; my heart and flesh sing for joy to the living God" (Ps. 84:1–2)? If not, I challenge you to take your spiritual preparation for corporate worship more seriously. Take the time and trouble to get yourself ready to worship the Lord and fellowship with the saints.

What you put into something determines what you will get out of it. This is even true of worship. Worshipers leave church silently complaining that they did not get anything out of it. Just as often, their complaints label blame for why the service was not better. The preacher did this. The musicians and singers did not do that. Or someone else did or did not do the other. Yet complainers rarely consider the service may not have been more meaningful because they were present and absent at the same time.

The best time to begin these preparations is Saturday night, not Sunday morning. It has been a long week. Between family commitments, work responsibilities, or school assignments, you have little time for yourself. Saturdays may be the only day you can get some rest, run needed errands, and enjoy a little recreation.

I understand. And I encourage you to take full advantage of the limited and precious opportunities Saturdays provide you to slow down or catch up. But Sunday is not technically part of the "weekend." It is the first day of the week. Sunday is the Lord's Day! It is the day the church has biblically and historically met to worship the Lord.

HOW DO YOU COME TO WORSHIP?

Be marked present for worship on the Lord's Day. But do not show up just to say you were there. Be prepared to participate fully. Peter exhorts, "So put away all malice and all deceit and hypocrisy and envy and all slander. Like newborn infants, long for the pure spiritual milk, that by it you may grow up into salvation—if indeed you have tasted that the Lord is good" (1 Peter 2:1–3). To change your appetite, change your attitude. Your desire for spiritual milk is ruined by sinful ways. You must lay aside any sinful ways to come to church with a good attitude and a big appetite.

Here's the bottom line. Sunday morning begins on Saturday nights.

Actually, it starts way before Saturday night. It starts on Monday. How we seek God, treat others, and govern ourselves all week affects Sunday morning. But Saturday night should be used strategically for the coming Sunday. You cannot rip and run all Saturday morning, pursue worldly things Saturday evening, stay up all Saturday night, and then get up on Sunday and shake all of that off for worship. Although you should take advantage of any free time Saturday provides, do so without forgetting you will begin your week in worship and fellowship with Christ and His body, the church.

The apostle Paul rebuked the church for abusing the Lord's Supper. The Corinthian saints received the body and blood of Christ in an unworthy manner and dishonored those who had nothing. These divisive acts were so severe that Paul claimed it was the reason some members of the church were sick and some had died (1 Cor. 11:30). As bad as these abuses were, however, Paul did not ban or bar anyone from the Lord's Table. Rather, Paul admonished, "Let a person examine himself, then, and so eat of the bread and drink of the cup" (1 Cor. 11:28).

When I get into a rhythm at work, it is easy for me to skip lunch. I can go all day without thinking about food. Then, as I drive home from the office, hunger attacks. I walk into the house to the smell of food my wife has cooked. As I start to grab a plate, Crystal says, "Don't you dare touch that food, Mr. Charles."

Her rebuke does not deny me a meal. She cooked the food for us to eat. It would offend her for us not to eat the meal she has prepared. When Crystal blocks me from getting a plate after I get home, I immediately leave the room to follow her unspoken instructions. I go to the bathroom and wash my hands. Then I return to the kitchen, fix myself a plate, and enjoy a good meal. It was not that I was unwelcome. It was that I am not allowed to come to the table with hands dirty from outside.

In a greater, deeper, higher way, the Lord has given us His body and blood. He bids us to eat and drink in remembrance of Him. We should not dishonor the Lord by coming to the table in an unworthy manner. We should seek to come before the Lord with clean hands and pure hearts. We should examine ourselves and then eat and drink of Christ. May I dare say that this call to examination, preparation, and consecration does not only apply to receiving the Lord's Table?

Examine yourself before you gather with the people of God.

Examine yourself before you make your petitions to God in prayer.

Examine yourself before you sing praise to God's glory.

Examine yourself before you sit under the Word of God.

Examine yourself before you give an offering to God.

Sunday mornings should be the best day of the week for Christians. But what happens on Sunday mornings is determined by what happens on Saturday night. What you get out of going to church is determined by what you put into it. Your spiritual preparation for worship determines your meaningful participation in worship. Prepare yourself for worship on Saturday night, so you can wake up on Sunday morning and sing, "I was glad when they said to me, 'Let us go to the house of the Lord!'" (Ps. 122:1).

Chapter 14

✝

THE PUBLIC READING
OF SCRIPTURE

As the year 2000 approached, Ray Pritchard and the Calvary Memorial Church of Oak Park, Illinois, marked the new millennium with a Bible reading marathon from Genesis 1 to Revelation 22. At 6:00 a.m. on December 28, the congregation began an unbroken reading of the Word of God until midnight, December 31.

Pritchard responded to media inquiries by explaining that they read through the Scriptures to proclaim their confidence that the Bible is true. And every portion of Scripture deserves to be read and believed. They also wanted the world to know that the biblical message that carried the church for two thousand years would carry it forward, no matter what the future holds. This special event should be the normative practice of the church. In too many instances, this is not the case.

I have noted a decline in both congregational singing and Bible reading in worship in my travels over the years. I am glad to report that I have seen the lack of congregational singing turn around. More churches are singing together, rather than being sung to with special music. Even where the congregational singing is not done well, it is moving to see churches make an effort to sing together.

However, I have not seen much recovery of Bible reading in worship. Scripture is sometimes used to introduce the next song. Or a few verses are read to get the preacher started, then abandoned for whatever motivational insights he has to share. But it seems we have abandoned the independent public reading of Scripture as a regular element of corporate worship.

Worship services are filled with creative elements these days. Various ministry emphases. Hallmark-inspired holidays. Orchestrated dance routines. Multimedia presentations. But if special elements crowd out biblical elements, you are doing it wrong.

THE POWER OF THE WORD OF GOD

Exodus 24 records Israel's confirmation of their covenant with God. The confirmation took place in what can only be described as a worship service. The reading of the Word was central to this holy assembly (Ex. 24:3–8). Moses later commanded that the law of God be read in full to all of Israel every seven years (Deut. 31:9–13). After Israel crossed into Canaan, Joshua obeyed Moses's command and gathered the people of Israel to hear the reading of the words of the law (Josh. 8:30–35).

Nehemiah 8 records one of the great revivals in the Bible. Unlike the revival in Nineveh (Jonah 3), it was not sparked by prophetic preaching. Unlike contemporary "revivals," it was not initiated by a preacher, orchestrated by a team, or characterized by theatrics. The revival at the Water Gate began when the people told Ezra to bring the Book of the Law (Neh. 8:1–2). The Word was read from morning to afternoon. Difficult passages were explained (Neh. 8:8). But it was the reading of the Word, not preaching, that convicted and converted the people of Israel.

When Jesus spoke at the synagogue in Nazareth, He began his message by reading from Isaiah 61 (Luke 4:16–21). Luke also notes Scripture reading as a regular part of the synagogue services in the days of the early church (Acts 13:15; 15:21). Paul instructed that his letters be read in the assembly of the local churches (Col. 4:16; 1 Thess. 5:27). John wrote, "Blessed is the one who reads aloud the words of this prophecy, and blessed are those who hear, and who keep what is written in it, for the time is near" (Rev. 1:3).

These are some of the many references that should move us to prioritize Scripture reading in worship. But one primary passage speaks directly to us. Paul instructed Timothy, "Until I come, devote yourself to the public reading of Scripture, to exhortation, to teaching" (1 Tim. 4:13).

As with all the Pastoral Epistles, these instructions are more than ministry advice from a mentor to a protégé. They contain a timeless truth for us to heed. In gathering for worship, we must read Scripture, exhort with the Scriptures, and teach the Scriptures. Too many churches only follow two of these three instructions. In biblical preaching, we explain and apply the Word of God. But we do not take the command to read the Word seriously. To the degree this is the case at our local church, we should repent of our sin and change our ways.

THE CENTRALITY OF THE WORD OF GOD

The Word of God is to be the centerpiece of Christian worship. We should sing, pray, and preach the Scriptures. But none of these essential elements should replace the reading of Scripture. It is a gross contradiction that pastors and churches seek to encounter and experience God in worship but fail to let God speak in the worship service by reading His Word. The songs and sermons may or may not rightly reflect God's Word. But God speaks clearly, purely, and authoritatively through the simple reading of His Word. The pastoral leaders and gathered church should devote themselves to the public reading of Scripture.

I do not believe 1 Timothy 4:13 merely means that we should read Scripture before or during the sermon. Without a doubt, Scripture should be read in the sermon. If I may add a footnote on preaching here, I believe Scripture should be read before the sermon begins. It is the custom of some preachers to introduce the sermon before reading the text. As long as you get to the text, that's fine. But it makes a greater statement to read Scripture first as foundational to what will be said in the sermon.

Beyond the sermon, the Word of God should be read as an independent element in the service. And it should not necessarily be directly tied to the sermon. If the sermon is from an Old Testament passage, read a New Testament passage. And don't just read a couple of verses. Read a long enough passage to demonstrate your confidence in the authority and clarity of Scripture. Does your church preach the Scriptures consecutively? How about reading them sequentially, as well? Pick a book of the Bible and read through a portion of it each Sunday.

Paul's instruction to read Scripture publicly (1 Tim. 4:13) is not a contrast to the private Scripture reading. It emphasizes that Scripture should be read aloud. As such, Scripture should be read well! Much planning and preparation go into the music, preaching, and other elements. The Word of God should not be read haphazardly.

Select those who can read well for the vital ministry of Scripture reading. (This is so crucial that, with rare exceptions, a pastoral leader or trainee should read the Word to the congregation.) Make sure the one who reads has the chance to familiarize himself with the Scripture to understand what he reads. Get a sense of the terrain, truth, and tone of the passage. Then practice reading through the text aloud multiple times. Work through hard-to-read words or phrases. Pause at all commas; stop at all periods. Get a Bible with large enough font to see. Read the Word loudly and clearly.

The practical advice in the previous paragraph by no means suggests that the one who reads the Scripture should put on a show. The content of the reading, not the ability of the reader, should draw the congregation's attention. But the Word of God should be read as the Word of God! In our church, the congregation stands when Scripture is read to honor the divine Author of the Scriptures. We want even our physical posture to reflect our reverent attitude toward God's Word. Standing or sitting, we should not read Scripture casually, like reading a newspaper. Read Scripture as an act of worship so that the congregation will hear it an act of worship to the glory of God.

Chapter 15

THE MINISTRY OF MUSIC

I preached a citywide meeting years ago. The host church provided the music. The director stood the choir, called up the lead singer, and readied the musicians. Before the music began, the choir quoted Colossians 3:16 in unison: "Let the word of Christ dwell in you richly, teaching and admonishing one another in all wisdom, singing psalms and hymns and spiritual songs, with thankfulness in your hearts to God." Then the music began, and the choir sang.

I sat in utter shock. I had never seen that before. I haven't seen it since that night. After the service, I asked the pastor about it. He explained there were nagging problems in his music department. He had to sit the choir down for a period. He only permitted them to sing again after teaching extensively on biblical worship. When the revamped ensemble resumed singing, they started quoting Colossians 3:16 to remind themselves and the congregation of their role in worship. I do not propose that singers recite Colossians 3:16 before every set of music. But this verse should govern the choices, priorities, motives, and conduct of the worship leaders.

Colossians 3:16 commands Christians and congregations to let the Word of Christ dwell in us richly. The Word of God should not come and go, show up occasionally, or be a vacation spot visited on special occasions. It should dwell in us richly. God's Word should feel at home in us. It should have the run of the house.

This verse affirms the critical role music in worship plays in the spiritual formation, gospel nurturing, and Christlike development of the saints. But what this verse says about music in worship is only understood in the context of its command to let the Word of Christ dwell in us richly. Christian worship should be Word-driven. When worship is Word-driven, it will be God-exalting, not man-centered.

SCRIPTURE-DRIVEN MUSIC

In many churches, music and preaching are in conflict and competition. But the music is to partner, to be an extension of the ministry of the Word. They are distinct but united elements of Christian worship.

Some churches refer to the musical sets as "Praise and Worship." This is not a good way to describe this time. If the fifteen or twenty minutes of music is praise and worship, what are we doing the rest of the service? Worship does not end when the music is over. The music should set the stage for the highest act of Christian worship: preaching and hearing the Word of God.

At the same time, it is wrong to think that the teaching does not start until the music ends. Colossians 3:16 urges us to teach and admonish one another in all wisdom by singing psalms and hymns and spiritual songs. The choir is teaching as it sings just as much as the preacher teaches during the sermon. The typical congregation may remember the leader's song long after it has forgotten the preacher's outline. The melody embeds lyrics in our minds, whether it teaches truth or error. What stewardship! The pastor should be rebuked if he teaches error in his sermon. And the singers should be rebuked if they teach error in their songs.

PASTOR-LED MUSICAL PRAISE

The teaching pastor is the worship leader of the church. The pastor's public ministry of prayer and the ministry of the Word (Acts 6:4) includes shepherding the selection of music in worship. He may not be able to sing. He may not play an instrument. He may not know much about music. But the pastor must not abandon his responsibility to promote and defend sound doctrine, including what is taught as the church sings. I repeat: music in worship is an extension of the ministry of the Word.

There is actually no such thing as "Christian music." There are only Christian lyrics. The emphasis should always be on the lyrics, not the music that accompanies it. Colossians 3:16 exhorts us to teach one another with psalms, hymns, and spiritual songs.

"Psalms" were probably songs taken directly from the Old Testament book of Psalms.

"Hymns" were most likely songs of praise that taught and affirmed Christian truth. Philippians 2:5–11 and Colossians 1:15–20 may be early Christian hymns.

Music in worship is an extension of the ministry of the Word.

"Spiritual songs" may have been songs of praise that emphasize personal testimony of the goodness of God.

Ultimately, we do not know the difference between psalms, hymns, and spiritual songs. Any hard distinction between these musical styles is purely speculative. But the point is not what these terms mean in distinction from one another. The point is that together these terms describe the rich variety of music that should be used in Christian worship. The Lord does not dislike a particular song or style because you don't like it. God likes any music that helps the Word of Christ dwell in us richly. It has nothing to do with musical styles, leaders, or groups. The concern is that the content of the songs facilitates the ministry of the Word.

None of this suggests that only the words count in worship music. Colossians 3:16 says we should sing psalms, hymns, and spiritual songs with thankfulness in our hearts to God. Our singing is to proclaim the truth of God's grace and celebrate the experience of God's grace. And it should come from the heart. It does not matter how beautiful your voice is, God is not honored if your singing is not the overflow of your heart's devotion.

In another place, Paul wrote, "And do not get drunk with wine, for that is debauchery, but be filled with the Spirit, addressing one another in psalms and hymns and spiritual songs, singing and making melody to the Lord with your heart" (Eph. 5:18–19).

This passage blows my mind every time I consider it. But Scripture plainly says the evidence of being Spirit-filled is that He will put a song in your heart. No, being Spirit-filled will not make you a singer. If you cannot sing before you are Spirit-filled, you still can't sing once you are Spirit-filled. You will have a song in your heart, but the song will not be for you. We sing for one another. Spirit-filled Christians do not sing to show off, puff themselves up, or display their talents. We sing to build up one another in the faith.

Moreover, we sing to the Lord. Why do we sing? Ephesians 5:19–20 answers: "singing and making melody to the Lord with your heart, giving thanks always and for everything to God the Father in the name of our Lord Jesus Christ." Thanksgiving is essential to worship. We should give thanks to God unceasingly: "always." David determined, "I will bless the LORD at all times; his praise shall continually be in my mouth" (Ps. 34:1). We should also give thanks to God unconditionally: "for everything." First Thessalonians 5:18 exhorts: "Give thanks in all circumstances." But Ephesians 5:20 says we should give thanks *for* everything!

We sing in grateful praise to God for all He has done for us in Christ. Isaiah declared, "Sing praises to the LORD, for he has done gloriously; let this be made known in all the earth. Shout, and sing for joy, O inhabitant of Zion, for great in your midst is the Holy One of Israel" (Isa. 12:5–6). All things should be done decently and in order in worship. But the goal of the service is not to maintain control. It is to offer worship. The Lord is worthy of uninhibited praise! The Word and worship go together. To know God is to praise God!

Chapter 16

✝

LET THE CHURCH SAY AMEN

For many years, I preached a Holy Week meeting in Detroit. One year, I walked to the pulpit and exhorted the church, "Let's give the Lord a hand of praise!" It was a new thing for me. I had heard one of my favorite preachers give this exhortation on many occasions. And, well, I thought it was cool. So I began to try it out when I stood to preach and greeted the congregation.

My appeal was greeted that night with mostly blank stares and awkward silence. The scattered handclaps only made the moment more awkward. The next night, I stood to preach with the same opening sentence. Same response. It happened again the next night. I thought the lack of response to my call for "hand praise" was strange in this warm congregation. But I was oblivious to the fact that something larger was going on.

During one service, the pastor led the congregation in singing. The members began to spontaneously clap as they sang. Over the singing, the pastor said, "That's how you give the Lord a hand clap of praise." Ouch.

The pastor never said anything to me directly about the matter. He did not need to. I'm a quick learner. I would soon abandon my newfound exhortation altogether.

For the record, there is nothing wrong with clapping your hands in praise to the Lord. Scripture commands it: "Clap your hands, all peoples! Shout to God with loud songs of joy!" (Ps. 47:1). There is a place for physical expression in worship. But there is a fine line between clapping as worship and clapping for worship.

Do you get the difference?

If the music ends and the congregation responds with applause, is it clear whether they are praising the Lord for the message of the song or showing appreciation for the musicians and singers who have just ministered to them? Worship should not celebrate spiritual gifts or the skills and talents of gifted people. Our worship should glorify the Father of Lights, who is the source of every good and perfect gift (James 1:17). Worship leaders lead the congregation in worship; they do not worship up front for the congregation's applause and appreciation.

A CONGREGATIONAL AMEN

How can you keep the focus on the Lord in worship? Let the church say "amen."

"Amen" means, "So be it." It is a word of confirmation that states approval, assurance, or affirmation. The term is one of the rare biblical words carried from the Old Testament Hebrew into the New Testament. And it means the same in all languages. In the Old Testament, the Israelites affirmed the truth of God in worship by saying "amen," not by clapping. It is the proper response to God-talk in worship. In the Old and New Testaments, the term is most often used to affirm praise to God, either by those who speak it or those who hear it.

During the revival at the Water Gate, Ezra the scribe blessed the Lord, the great God. In response, the people answered, "Amen,

Amen," lifting up their hands (Neh. 8:6). Note that the physical expression of uplifted hands was secondary and supplemental to the verbal affirmation of the praiseworthy truth about God that Ezra declared. The primary instrument of worship is the voice, not the organ, piano, guitar, or drums. The redeemed of the Lord should say so (Ps. 107:2).

In the New Testament, many benedictions and doxologies conclude with "amen" (Rom. 11:36; Eph. 3:21; Phil. 4:20; Heb. 13:21; 1 Peter 4:11). Remarkably, Scripture not only says "amen" to God, but it also uses the term to describe God. When Isaiah called God "the God of truth" (Isa. 65:16), he calls God "the God of Amen." Paul declared, "For all the promises of God find their Yes in him. That is why it is through him that we utter our Amen to God for his glory" (2 Cor. 1:20). We should joyfully utter amen to the glory of the Lord Jesus Christ.

One Sunday, I preached for a Presbyterian friend. The time of worship was wonderful but also strange for me for several reasons. I often preach away from home. But I am not usually out of my pulpit on Sunday mornings. It was a rare time my wife and children were able to travel with me. And it was the first time my Baptist family attended a Presbyterian church. That last factor did not dawn on me until I started preaching. Throughout the sermon, the excellent acoustics carried Crystal's voice throughout the room. "Amen." "Talk, sir." "Preach it!" I counted it a victory that an usher did not come down the aisle and escort my wife out of the service.

PASTOR AND CONGREGATION IN AGREEMENT

On a serious note, I understand that many churches would find it disruptive to have a lone voice crying out "Amen" in the middle of the service. I don't think it would necessarily be a bad thing. I do get that it can be viewed as a distraction or disruption. But could the pastoral leaders consider the appropriateness of a congregational Amen?

Inevitably, times of prayer are part of worship services at your local church. Most likely, whoever leads the prayer ends by saying "amen." It is not an unofficial way of indicating the prayer is over. In a real sense, the closing Amen is a closing petition: "May it be so." How does your congregation respond when the prayer is over? How should the congregation respond? The proper response is for the assembly to say "amen."

The person leading the corporate prayer is not just praying for the congregation; he is praying with the congregation. As the pastor prays audibly, the congregation is to be praying along with him silently. When the pastor finishes the prayer, the congregation should indicate their agreement with what was just prayed by saying "amen." It expresses unity in prayer, harmony with the petitions made, and even encouragement to the one who led the prayer.

When a hymn or song of praise is concluded, worship leaders often issue a post-song call to praise. To be honest, this can undermine the church's congregational singing, when we suggest that the praise and worship happen in response to the song rather than during the singing. But if there is to be a post-song call to praise, what if it were a call for the congregation to say, "amen"? If the song is to or about the Lord, there should be more than invoked emotions. Truth should be proclaimed. Allow the church to affirm the gospel truth of the song by saying Amen.

> **Saying "amen" to a preacher is like saying "sic 'em" to a dog! Beyond encouraging the pray-er, saying amen communicates agreement with the truth.**

When I was a boy, the pulpit would encourage the pew to give the preacher their ears, prayers, and amens. I still believe all three are significant. Saying "amen" to a preacher is like saying "sic 'em" to a dog! Beyond encouraging the pray-er, saying amen communicates agreement with the truth. In this sense, the congregation preaches with the preacher as he preaches to the congregation. We do not so much say "amen" to the preacher as we say "amen" to God in worshipful response to the preached truth.

A congregation quietly listening to the sermon is a powerful symbol of submission to the authority of God's Word. But don't forget the sermon is a part of the worship service, not Sunday school! The preacher should never forget that preaching the Word is an act of worship. And the congregation should never forget that the hearing of the Word is also an act of worship. The saints should receive the truth and respond to it. Your congregation may never be as loud and talkative as the spirited black worship in the church where I serve. Can it be more participatory than it is currently?

Let the church say "amen."

Chapter 17

✝

THE CHURCH IS NOT A HOTEL

It is never a light matter for a pastor to invite another pastor into his pulpit to preach to his congregation. For this reason, I am grateful for every speaking invitation I receive. And I count it a privilege to minister the Word outside of my local church.

However, I do not like the travel part of traveling to speak. The airports. The flights. The hotels. There is nothing glamorous about any of it. These are work trips. I go to fulfill my assignment, then I return home as soon as possible. After I am wheels down in Jacksonville, I often post a one-word tweet: "Home."

I enjoy being at home with my wife and kids.

I am most comfortable in my normal routine of daily activities.

I am most productive in my study, surrounded by my library.

When I return home after a trip, it does not take long or take much for me to get the road out of my system. At least, I think it is out of my system until, at some point, my wife says, "I don't know where you think you are, Mr. Charles. But this is not a hotel."

I have been on the working end of this not-so-subtle admonition on many occasions. Yet I am genuinely surprised every time I hear it. "What did I do?" I ask, cluelessly. Then Crystal points out some domestic sin I have committed unawares. I made a mess and left it for someone else to pick up, as if I assumed housekeeping would clean up after me. I suddenly announced I was hungry, as if I was ready to order room service to be delivered. I used a washcloth and bath towel once and then got a new one, as if I expected newly washed and folded towels to be restocked daily.

My dear wife watches this routine as long as she can, until she has to remind me that I am not in a hotel. I am a resident of this home. I am a member of this family. I am a part of this household.

Of course, this is not breaking news to me. I know that my home is not a hotel. Yet the subtle dynamics of road life can quickly spoil you. You order what you want to eat, rather than eating what is prepared for you. You do not have to share the remote control with anyone. You receive the service of others with no obligation to participate.

It does not have to be five-star treatment, either. The simplest accommodations provide many luxuries that can easily be taken for granted. Then the rhythms of home life force you back into the real world. The rhythms of corporate worship in a local church should accomplish the same thing for the spoiled Christian. We should participate in our local church as members of the household, not guests.

The apostle Peter made this point to persecuted Christians in the Roman province of Asia Minor. With all the troubles these saints faced, Peter did not point them to the church to receive benefits from the ministry of others. He reminded them of their household duties as members of the church. Peter exhorted, "As each has received a gift, use it to serve one another, as good stewards of God's varied grace" (1 Peter 4:10).

THE PURPOSE OF GOD'S GIFTS

It is not right, good, or wise for the church to put so-called gifted people on a pedestal. Each and every Christian has been gifted to serve. There is no such thing as an ungifted Christian. No Christian has all the gifts, and no Christian is without a gift. The Lord has graciously equipped and enabled every Christian for ministry to others. We are saved to serve.

What is my gift?

How can I discover my gift?

Do I have more than one gift?

These are big questions. Peter ignored them all. The apostle asserted that every believer has been gifted by God. He then skipped the whole discussion about how to find one's gifts. Assuming every Christ-follower has received a gift, he exhorted us to use them to serve one another. Could this be Peter's explanation for how to find your gift? Get busy serving one another. You do not discover your gift through ministry assessments. You discover your gifts through ministry deployment. It is easier to steer a car that is in motion. And it is easier to find your spiritual gift in the act of service. Find a need and meet it. As you serve, the Holy Spirit and your local congregation will affirm your gifts.

> **You do not discover your gift through ministry assessments. You discover your gifts through ministry deployment.**

Peter also made a subtle but significant statement about the nature of spiritual gifts. We are to use them to serve one another. Spiritual gifts are tools to work with, not toys to play with. No gift is given for self-edification. Your gift is for others.

We are gifted by God to serve one another. "One another" affirms the priority of the church. Our gifts are not to entertain the world. They are to edify the saints. "So then," wrote Paul, "as we have opportunity, let us do good to everyone, and especially to those who are of the household of faith" (Gal. 6:10).

With the gifts God gives us, we should serve one another as "stewards of God's varied grace" (1 Peter 4:10). Christian service is a fundamental element of total-life stewardship (see chapter 8). At the final inspection (2 Cor. 5:10), we will give account for our stewardship of the gifts the Lord has given us to serve others. Your service in and to the household of faith is not optional. It is a God-given duty with eternal ramifications. You can refuse to be account-able to the leaders and members of your local church. But you will give account to the Lord for your participation in the body life of the church.

First Peter 4 is the last of three key passages about spiritual gifts. Romans 12 and 1 Corinthians 12 record lists of spiritual gifts. Peter did not give a list. He placed spiritual gifts in two categories: "who-ever speaks, as one who speaks oracles of God; whoever serves, as one who serves by the strength that God supplies" (1 Peter 4:11). All spiritual gifts fall into two categories: speaking gifts and serv-ing gifts. Some serve by speaking. Others serve without speaking. Titles, offices, and positions are not mentioned. The emphasis is on the function, not the role.

MINISTRY OF GOD'S GIFTS

If you minister by speaking, be it private counsel or public teaching, you are to speak God's Word, not your advice. Here is an-other reminder that everything that happens in the church should be an extension of the ministry of the Word. Be it singing in the congregation, teaching in a Bible study group, or personal encour-agement in the lobby, the ministry of speech should be the ministry of Scripture.

If you minister by serving, be it in some obvious role up front or an unseen task behind the scenes, serve by the strength God supplies. You should cook a meal, park a car, or operate a sound board by the power of God. No act of service should be done in our strength, wisdom, or resources. The simplest act of ministry service should be done with humble dependence upon divine help.

Why serve? Why devote yourself to building up other saints? Why treat the church as a household and not a hotel? First Peter 4:10 gives two reasons. We are to serve one another because we have been gifted to serve. We serve one another because we are stewards of grace. Verse 11 gives an additional reason, the ultimate reason we should serve one another: "in order that in everything God may be glorified through Jesus Christ. To him belong glory and dominion forever and ever. Amen."

Speak by God's Word, so that when someone is helped by what you say, the Lord will get the glory. Serve by God's strength, so that when someone is helped by what you do, the Lord will get the glory. Warren Wiersbe wrote, "Ministry takes place when divine resources meet human needs through loving channels to the glory of God."[7] God meets needs. We are only channels. To be a channel God uses, do all to the glory of God (1 Cor. 10:31).

Chapter 18

LITTLE SCREENS AND CORPORATE WORSHIP

My local movie theater had a new "silence your cellphones" announcement. It stated that you came to the theater to enjoy what is on the big screen, and you should not allow the little screen on your phone to make you forget what you came to see on the big screen. The movie is not the time for selfies, text messages, or social media. It is time to drink a cola, eat a tub of popcorn, and enjoy the happenings on the big screen in front of you.

Movies are for entertainment. It may be a comedy, drama, horror, historical, adventure, fantasy, or action flick. But the goal is that you leave the theater entertained. It's all about having a good time. Yet theaters think what is happening is important enough to ask us to stay off our phones while the movie is playing. Is this too much to ask when we go to church to worship Christ?

Our cellphones, tablets, and other electronic devices constantly add fun and practical functions. As a result, some do not feel the need to come to church with anything but an iPad. Their Bibles, study resources, prayer lists, journals for note-taking, and apps of their favorite preachers' sermons are on their tablet. And they don't need an envelope anymore; they can give an offering through their cellphone.

The apps on our devices make life so much easier. They can also make worship more difficult. If you are not careful, smartphones and tablets will distract you from the truth, fellowship, and service that should characterize corporate worship.

Social media is a great way to connect with family and friends. We instinctively share with our "friends" and "followers" the things that catch our interest throughout the day. This instinct naturally continues when we are in corporate worship. As we are being blessed in worship, we immediately share it on Twitter, Facebook, or Instagram. If something silly or surprising happens in worship, we do the same.

Is this a good thing?

Let me say it again, for the people in the back. I am not condemning all use of phones or tablets in worship. The barn door is already open on this one. And I am okay with that. I will not spend this chapter arguing that you should not bring your device to church. I'm sure you have already made up your mind. However, I want to appeal to you to use personal technology in corporate worship with care, concern, and caution. The convenience of technological devices can quickly and easily become a distraction in worship.

> **The convenience of technological devices can quickly and easily become a distraction in worship.**

DISTRACTED FROM GOD'S WORD

While attending a convention, I decided not to take my Bible to the next session. I would use the Bible app on my phone. "It's a convention meeting, not Sunday morning worship," I reasoned. When the sermon began, I opened to the biblical text to follow along. But a temptation arose that I couldn't resist. I just had to know if I had received any new emails.

I was not going to respond to any emails, but I just had to check. I could not tell you what the preacher was saying to save my life. Then I was abruptly snapped back to attention. "Young man," the mother sitting next to me whispered, "you need to put that phone away and hear the Word of God!" Ouch!

I love the convenience of my phone and tablet. But is this a good thing when I am tempted to multitask in worship?

A lot of Christians struggle in their private devotions during the week. For many, Sunday mornings are the only time the Lord gets their undivided attention. How does that work when there is a strong and easily fulfilled temptation to text, email, or web surf during worship? On Saturday night, a person may do sinful things on his tablet. On Sunday morning, that person uses that tablet as a Bible in worship. Isn't there something inappropriate about that? Something that would not happen if that person simply used a Bible on Sunday morning?

I am old enough to remember when churches began using streaming services. Not too many years later, anyone with a smartphone can go live at any moment. When we should be ministering to God or one another, we go live on our social media platforms. In so doing, we go from being participants in worship to producers of media content.

Is this good?
Is this wise?
Is this helpful?
Is this edifying?
Is this worship?

I am raising questions I do not have all the answers to. I do not have a list of solutions to offer. But I do issue this warning: do whatever it takes to make sure that the convenience of technology does not become a distraction in worship.

RECORDING AND EDITING WORSHIP

I am becoming increasingly convinced that when we start sharing or recording the moment, we are no longer worshiping God. Worship is our response to God's intoxicating worthiness. Worship happens as we forget about ourselves and are consumed with the greatness of God. How do you stand in awe of God and share the moment on social media at the same time? Your need to commune with God in worship should not be undermined by the possibility that someone will benefit from seeing it later on social media.

The worship service is blessing you. You don't want to be selfish. So you grab your phone and capture the moment to share with your friends and followers later. But this selfless act is actually very selfish. Your concern for friends on social media ignores the family you are sitting with in worship! We have a "one another" responsibility to our brothers and sisters in Christ.

Movie theaters adopt cellphone policies with a clear agenda. They want to make money, maintain customers, and increase revenues. Moviegoers are increasingly staying away from theaters because cellphone use ruins the experience. Arguments and fights have broken out when someone is asked to turn off their phone. Movie theaters have their own concerns, which are not Christ-exalting or kingdom focused. This is all the more reason for us to treat the worship of Christ with greater honor than theaters have for their latest tentpole feature.

Corporate worship is not a public version of your prayer closet.

In corporate worship, the church should be "all with one accord in one place" (Acts 2:1 NKJV). The worship service is a family dinner at a fine restaurant, not a fast-food meal on your couch in front of the TV. Worship etiquette should be practiced out of reverence for God and respect for your fellow worshipers.

Pastors must lead the way. In corporate worship, we should point our congregations away from the ever-present technology that dominates so much of our lives. Many church members go all week without spending time in prayer and Scripture. They have too many things distracting them. What makes you think those distractions can facilitate true worship on Sunday mornings? True worship is to look up! How can you teach your people to humbly rejoice in the transcendence of God when you are taking congregational selfies in the pulpit?

I may be an old fogey who just needs to get with the times. Technology is here to stay. It will only grow more prevalent as time goes by. It is unrealistic to think these realities will have no bearing on corporate worship. But there are big questions every believer and congregation should wrestle with.

Where do you draw the line?

At what point does the use of technology morph the worship service into something else?

Is a movie theater more sacred than the house of worship?

Chapter 19

✝

➤ ➤ ➤   ◄ ◄ ◄

VACATION AND CORPORATE WORSHIP

Jesus sent the twelve apostles on a short-term mission trip to preach the gospel, heal the sick, and cast out demons (Mark 6:7–13). After some unspecified time, the disciples returned and reported to Jesus the message they proclaimed and the miracles they performed (Mark 6:30). Following their report, Jesus said to the disciples, "Come away by yourselves to a desolate place and rest a while" (Mark 6:31).

This is a beautiful picture of the concern, gentleness, and wisdom of Jesus. After the disciples gave their report, Jesus did not grade their efforts. He did not use this as an opportunity to teach and train the disciples. And the Lord did not immediately give them their next ministry assignment. Jesus was more concerned about the toll their ministry efforts had on them. So He invited them to get away from the crowd, retreat to a quiet place, and rest from their labors.

The Lord's concern for His first disciples is the Lord's concern for all of His disciples. But Mark 6:31 is about more than taking vacations. Jesus called His disciples to rest after they wore themselves out doing kingdom business.

This verse is not merely a call to take a break from your worldly pursuits. It is a spiritual challenge: When is the last time you wore yourself out ministering to others in the name of the Lord? Unfortunately, many churches exist by the 80/20 principle: 20 percent of the members do 80 percent of the work. That is not the way it is supposed to be in the church.

Paul said, "Therefore, my beloved brothers, be steadfast, immovable, always abounding in the work of the Lord, knowing that in the Lord your labor is not in vain" (1 Cor. 15:58). May the Lord fill our congregations with saints who are so busy for the Lord that He bids them to come apart and rest a while.

The apostles retreated from the crowd to a quiet place *with* Jesus. Vacations are a needed time of rest and relaxation. This break from the various responsibilities of home, work, or school is a good thing. However, there is no such thing as a vacation, leave of absence, or sabbatical from following Christ. Take a vacation whenever you can. But do not take a vacation from Jesus. Your vacation should never involve locations, company, or activities that exclude Jesus. "And whatever you do, in word or deed, do everything in the name of the Lord Jesus, giving thanks to God the Father through him" (Col. 3:17).

Jesus' invitation to His disciples to "Come away . . . and rest a while" also applies to present-day disciples. Your life in Christ is supernatural. It is not superhuman. If you do not come apart, you will fall apart. All of us need times of rest, relaxation, and rejuvenation. But remember that Christ's call to His disciples to come away was a call to go with Him to rest, not to go without Him.

How can you vacation to the glory of God?

ATTEND CORPORATE WORSHIP ON THE LORD'S DAY

You have carefully planned your vacation months in advance. You have big plans with family and friends. You have great expectations of a memorable trip. Airplane tickets? Check. Hotel accommodations? Check. Car rental? Check. Local church? Wait. Huh? You haven't thought about going to church during your vacation? You should. Church attendance should be a consideration you factor in as you make vacation plans.

Hebrews 10:24–25 also applies to your summer vacation: "And let us consider how to stir up one another to love and good works, not neglecting to meet together, as is the habit of some, but encouraging one another, and all the more as you see the Day drawing near." Make every effort to find a Christ-centered, Bible-believing, gospel-preaching church with whom to worship King Jesus on the Lord's Day, wherever you are. As you have made plans for food, lodging, entertainment, and other things you deem important, make plans for corporate worship. You found a hotel to stay in. Find a church to go to. Be marked present on the Lord's Day.

FINANCIALLY SUPPORT YOUR LOCAL CHURCH

"Staycations" are becoming increasingly popular. A staycation is a vacation at home without the travel, hustle and bustle, or expenses. In most instances, however, your vacation will require you to travel. And the travel will cost you money. There is nothing wrong with this. If you work hard, plan wisely, and save strategically, you have every right to enjoy your vacation times. But your vacation should cost you, not the Lord.

Solomon counseled, "Honor the LORD with your wealth and with the firstfruits of all your produce; then your barns will be filled with plenty, and your vats will be bursting with wine" (Prov. 3:9–10).

The Lord generously provides for the needs of His people. The Lord does not provide resources for us to waste on worldly things. Honor the Lord with your possessions. The most fundamental way we honor the Lord with our wealth is by giving our firstfruits to Him. The Lord is not honored when we give to Him after we spend our finances on our bills, wants, and goals. Give to the Lord what is first, not what is last.

Your vacation should not become an excuse to dishonor God with your finances. Avoid putting yourself in debt for the sake of a few days of recreation. Enjoy yourself but stay within your means. And continue to financially support the ongoing work of the church that goes on while you are on vacation. Don't rob God, and don't rob yourself by wasting your resources and missing your opportunity to invest in the kingdom (Matt. 6:19–21).

SPEND TIME ON THINGS WITH ETERNAL VALUE

Your vacation is a wonderful opportunity to get some rest, enjoy your favorite hobbies, catch up on personal reading, try some new adventure, or just hang out with family and friends. All of these things have their place. But how often have you said that you would pray more or read the Word of God more if you had the time? How often have you thought, felt, or said you would do something for the Lord if you had the time? How often have you heard or read about opportunities to serve at church, and wish your schedule permitted you to participate?

Your vacation is an opportunity to serve the Lord. You do not have to spend all your time doing ministry. Are you willing to spend *any* of your time doing ministry? "Look carefully then how you walk, not as unwise but as wise, making the best use of the time, because the days are evil. Therefore do not be foolish, but understand what the will of the Lord is" (Eph. 5:15–17). We are living in evil days that call for us to walk in wisdom. Redeem the time. Make the best use of your time. Buy up every opportunity you can to serve the Lord with gladness.

ENJOY YOURSELF

The recommendations I have given in this chapter may seem radical to you. But I am not suggesting your vacation should be a short-term mission trip. Your vacation should be a vacation. Enjoy yourself! That's an order. Have a good time on your vacation. Enjoy the Lord's goodness to you. Don't feel guilty about it. And do not let anyone lay a guilt trip on you. God is not against you having a good time. God is the One who gives us life and breath and all things (Acts 17:25). God is the ultimate source of every good and perfect gift (James 1:17). God richly provides us with everything to enjoy (1 Tim. 6:17).

Friend, God is not some cosmic killjoy, determined to stop everyone from having a good time. The Lord is not against pleasure. But He is against those who are lovers of pleasure rather than lovers of God (2 Tim. 3:4). So enjoy the blessings of the Lord, the graces of life, the fruit of your labor, the opportunity to travel, and the company of family and friends. But keep pleasure in its place. Do not prioritize the pleasures of life over the love of God. Or as 1 Corinthians 10:31 says, "So, whether you eat or drink, or whatever you do, do all to the glory of God." Vacation to the glory of God!

Chapter 20

> > > ✝ < < <

WHEN IT'S TIME TO LEAVE A CHURCH

Church hopping stunts faith development. You will not, cannot, grow in Christlikeness jumping from congregation to congregation based on your personal preferences. You need to plant your roots in a local church that you worship with for years, God willing. If you transfer your membership, there is a proper time and appropriate way to leave a church.

What are the legitimate reasons for leaving a church?

When is the right time to leave a church?

How should one leave one church to join another?

WRONG REASONS FOR LEAVING A CHURCH

Sin. Someone has sinned. Maybe it was a leader. Is this a good reason to leave? Not necessarily. It does not promote holiness to leave because of sin. There was gross sin in the church at Corinth. Paul commanded the church to deal with the sinning member, not leave the church (1 Cor. 5:9–13). When Paul bids the saints to "come out from among them," he was talking about the world, not the church (see 2 Cor. 6:14–18).

Disagreements over secondary doctrinal issues. Biblical convictions matter. But you should not die on every hill. Contend earnestly for the faith (Jude 3). But don't break fellowship over every disagreement about Scripture. Paul advised Timothy "not to quarrel about words, which does no good, but only ruins the hearers" (2 Tim. 2:14). He added, "But avoid irreverent babble, for it will lead people into more and more ungodliness" (2 Tim. 2:16).

Disunity. God hates those who sow discord among brothers (Prov. 6:16–19). Only those who love the brothers have a genuine assurance of salvation (1 John 3:14). Christians must preserve the unity of the Spirit in the bond of peace in Christ (Eph. 4:1–3). Don't jump ship because you cannot get along with others. You will only have the same problem at the next church. Ask Christ to help you "count others more significant than your[self]" (Phil. 2:3).

Personal offenses. Moving every time you are (or feel) wronged will only lead to multiple church transitions. Or you will remain at the fringes of the church, which is just as bad. Jesus said, "If your brother sins against you, go and tell him his fault, between you and him alone. If he listens to you, you have gained your brother" (Matt. 18:15). If he does not listen, turn up the pressure (Matt. 18:16–20).

Unwillingness to submit to authority. Aaron was more religious than Moses. Joshua was a better warrior. But the rod was in Moses's hand. Don't fight those the Lord puts in leadership over you. You should not sit under unbiblical, immoral, or abusive leadership, and there is a way to deal with disqualified leaders (1 Tim. 5:19–20). But do not handcuff your spiritual leaders to personal preferences, empty traditions, or unbiblical priorities. Be willing to follow leadership.

A low view of the church. No chapter and verse commands you to be a church member. But Scripture teaches by what it assumes, just as much as it teaches by what it commands. There is no biblical category for an "unchurched Christian." Christ is the head of the church. You cannot be connected to the head and disconnected from the body. Christ loves the church (Eph. 5:25–27). And to love Christ is to love what He loves.

Disregard for truth. Paul charged Timothy to preach the Word (2 Tim. 4:2). Then he warned, "For the time is coming when people will not endure sound teaching, but having itching ears they will accumulate for themselves teachers to suit their own passions, and will turn away from listening to the truth and wander off into myths" (2 Tim. 4:3–4). Don't let that be you. If you are under sound teaching and faithful preaching, for God's sake, stay put!

WHEN IT'S TIME TO LEAVE A CHURCH

A gospel reason. If the church you are a member of does not believe or teach the biblical gospel, you need to leave. Now! We are saved by grace through faith in Christ, plus or minus nothing. Salvation is God's free gift to those who trust the blood and righteousness of Christ. Anyone who teaches any other "gospel" is accursed (Gal. 1:6–9). And any church that embraces a false gospel is not a Christian church. Run for your life!

A doctrinal reason. You should leave a church when a church requires you to deny what you believe or believe what you deny. You have three critical responsibilities: (1) the duty to live by faith (Rom. 14:23), (2) the guarding of your conscience against sin (James 4:17), and (3) the command to test all things (1 Thess. 5:21–22). Do not treat doctrinal matters lightly. Remember that peace at the expense of truth is not peace.

A personal reason. There are many personal reasons for leaving a church. The most common is relocation. If you move to a different city, join a local church where you live. That was Phoebe's situation (Rom. 16:1–2). If your church is so far from your home that it becomes a convenient excuse to skip church, find a good church closer to home.

HOW TO LEAVE A CHURCH

Pray. Bathe the decision to leave a church in fervent prayer. Pray about your motives, duties, and relationships. Pray to guard your heart (Prov. 4:23). Pray for wisdom (James 1:5). Pray for submissiveness to God's will (Col. 1:9). Pray about it; don't talk about it. Loose talk about your unprocessed thoughts and feelings can sow discord.

Examine your motives. Why do you want to leave? I'm not talking about the politically correct reasons you will tell others. I am talking about the true motivations of your heart. Do you even know them? Ask God to search you (Ps. 139:23–24). Then be honest with yourself and with God. Be careful not to move for the wrong reasons.

Review your commitments. Do you serve in the church? Are you a leader? Will your move disrupt the ministry? Answer these questions prayerfully before you leave. If you have made commitments, do everything within your power to honor them. Put the honor of Christ ahead of yours. Push past unworthy quitting points (1 Cor. 15:58). Do not go AWOL from an assignment the Lord has given you.

Reconcile unresolved conflict. Don't leave a church because you are mad about something. Do not leave because someone has offended you. Be ready to forgive and eager for reconciliation. Remember that broken fellowship suspends true worship (Matt. 5:23–24).

Consider others. If your heart is right, you will feel the weight of how your potential move will injure or influence others. If you can leave without affecting anyone, you were not a good member. If your presence matters, consider how your absence will affect others (Phil. 2:4).

Find a new church first. The Father does not want His children to be spiritually homeless (Eph. 2:19). The Lord typically leads to a place, not just away from a place. You should be able to leave a spiritual forwarding address when you leave a church. And you should be able to go to your new church with a recommendation from your old church.

Have an exit interview. Talk to your pastor before you leave. Is he the reason you want to go? That's all the more reason to schedule a conversation. Hebrews 13:17 says, "Obey your leaders and submit to them, for they are keeping watch over your souls, as those who will have to give an account. Let them do this with joy and not with groaning, for that would be of no advantage to you."

Part 3:

LEADING
WORSHIP

Chapter 21

✝

➤ ➤ ➤   ◄ ◄ ◄

CALLING GOD'S PEOPLE TO WORSHIP

Imagine the scene.

You are an ancient Israelite. The time for one of the Jewish feasts draws near. In obedience to God's law, you make the pilgrimage to the holy city of Jerusalem. Your final destination is the temple. Your ultimate purpose is worship. Your consuming motivation is thanksgiving, grateful praise for all the Lord has done for you and your people.

The pilgrimage has caught up with you. When you left home, you were focused. You are now frustrated. Jerusalem is still many miles away. The journey is long; the sun is relentless. The path is uninviting, the sacrifice is burdensome, the caravan is noisy, and you find yourself repeatedly asking, *Why did I leave home for this?* You do not answer that question. You cannot answer it. Your mind is too far from worship. You would turn around and go home, but you are as far from home as you are from Jerusalem.

Then you hear a noise in the distance. No, it's not the clamor of the caravan. The noise you hear is melodic, harmonious, beautiful. You are nearing Jerusalem. Finally. And you are met by greeters.

These are not contemporary church greeters who welcome you with handshakes or hugs. It is a choir lifting a psalm of thanks: "Make a joyful noise to the LORD, all the earth! Serve the LORD with gladness! Come into his presence with singing!" (Ps. 100:1–2). As you hear their song, your nagging frustrations melt away. It's time to worship.

We live in very different times than the ancient Israelites sojourning to Jerusalem for the annual feasts. But we share some things in common. Each week, the members of our church make a pilgrimage to the place of worship. We make the trip with transportation, luxuries, and conveniences the ancients would have never dreamed of. But we know what it is to travel to worship with frustrations that distract us from the reason we are going to church. In many ways, we feel these frustrations more than Old Testament Israel did. All the more, the people of God need to be called to worship Him in spirit and truth.

A SACRED CALL

The "call to worship" is generally associated with more formal or liturgical worship services. But there is good reason for pastors and other worship leaders to make it a part of their weekly assembly, whether your services are formal or informal. Bryan Chapell wrote, "With a scriptural Call to Worship, God invites us by his Word to join the worship of the ages and angels. God does not simply invite us to a party of friends, or a lecture on religion, or a concert of sacred music—he invites us into the presence of the King of the Universe before whom all creation will bow and for whom all heaven now sings."[8]

Every church worship service starts one way or another. How the meeting begins sets the tone for what will take place. This is why services should start on time as scheduled. It is why there should be some strategic planning of the opening moments of the service. It is why the worship service should begin with a call to worship. While I'm here, let me say that worship should start and end well. Start the service with a call to worship. And end the service by praising God's glory in a doxology or announcing God's blessings in a benediction.

There are many good reasons to join the church where I serve. Our parking situation and building layout are not among them. We are blessed to worship God together in a beautiful room. But our parking lots are spread out, surrounding the building. And there are multiple entrances into the facility. You may have parked near a door, but that does not mean you are near the area of the building you are trying to get to. The trek from the parking lot to the nursery, your small group room, or the main auditorium may feel like the ancient Israelites' pilgrimage to Jerusalem.

It would be foolish to assume that when our members finally make it to their seats, they are ready and focused for worship. They need to be reminded why we have gathered. And it may not all come back to them when the songs, prayers, or sermon begins. By then, the service has moved on down the road. The members may try to catch up. In many instances, it will be too late. They will sit through the service respectfully. But their minds and hearts are a million miles from what's going on. They can only promise themselves they will do better next Sunday, God willing.

A MAJESTIC CALL

Three months after the Exodus, the Lord called a meeting with the newly freed slaves (Ex. 19). It would be the first formal meeting between the children of Israel and their Redeemer. Moses consecrated the people over the next three days to prepare the Israelites to meet with God. And they were given specific meeting protocols.

No one was to touch Mount Sinai, lest they die.

The Lord showed up to the meeting with thunder, lightning, thick clouds, and trumpet blasts. After this meeting, the frightened people said to Moses, "You speak to us, and we will listen; but do not let God speak to us, lest we die" (Ex. 20:19).

The blood and righteousness of Christ have opened for us a new and living way to God (Heb. 10:20). But our new access to God in Christ does not mean the nature or character of God has changed. Our God is a consuming fire (Heb. 12:29). Jesus taught us to approach God in prayer as "Our Father in heaven" (Matt. 6:9). But the first petition He taught us to pray to the heavenly Father is, "Hallowed be your name."

We should approach God in worship with reverence, humility, and submission. The pastor, or whoever is assigned to open the service, should make this clear up front. Don't begin the service by asking the congregation, "How are you feeling today?" Countdown clocks, rousing opening songs, or friendly words of welcome do not communicate the gravity of what is happening as we gather for worship. Find a way to say to the assembled worshipers, "Behold your God!"

The call to worship need not be sad or solemn. Psalm 100:4 beckons, "Enter his gates with thanksgiving, and his courts with praise! Give thanks to him; bless his name!" The worship of God should not be like waiting in a doctor's office, sitting in a traffic jam, or attending a funeral. Worship should be joyful. Etymologically, the word *enthusiasm* means "God within." Enthusiasm in worship should not be contrived or compelled. It should flow from hearts filled with love, hope, and joy in God.

As you call God's people to worship, resist the temptation to preach a sermonette. The call to worship should be brief, clear, and simple. Above all, it should be scriptural. No long speech is necessary. You can call the congregation to worship by reading an appropriate Scripture. A scriptural call to worship establishes God's initiative and authority in the service.

We do not gather because the church leaders instruct us to. We do not gather because this is what we traditionally do on Sundays. We do not gather because we feel like going to church this weekend. Psalm 106:1 says, "Praise the LORD! Oh give thanks to the LORD, for he is good; for his steadfast love endures forever!" We gather because the Word of God calls us to worship. It is not a worship experience. It is a worship service. We serve God in worship, not the other way around.

Chapter 22

✝

WORSHIP BEYOND COLOR LINES

Divine necessity compelled Jesus to travel to Galilee through Samaria. Weary from the journey, Jesus rested at Jacob's Well in Sychar as His disciples went for food. As He sat there, a woman from Samaria came to draw water. A life-changing conversation ensued. It started with a seemingly mundane discussion about water. Then the subject shifted from water to marriage, divorce, and remarriage. Then it moved from adultery to worship.

The woman said, "Sir, I perceive that you are a prophet. Our fathers worshiped on this mountain, but you say that in Jerusalem is the place where people ought to worship" (John 4:19–20). Many Bible commentators read this statement as a tactical diversion. It seems the woman tried to lure Jesus into a religious debate to shift the conversation away from her multiple divorces and adulterous affair. However, I believe this woman was genuinely convicted by the words of Jesus. She recognized her sinfulness. She wanted to get right with God. She understood this process required the offering of a sacrifice. But herein was the dilemma: What was the proper place to offer acceptable worship—on the mountain or in Jerusalem?

During a *Meet the Press* interview in 1960, Dr. Martin Luther King Jr. lamented that 11:00 on Sunday mornings is the most segregated hour in Christian America. More than sixty years later, that sad indictment remains true. Why? A key reason for racial segregation in the church in America is that we choose answers to questions about worship from the categories the woman at the well used.

We choose Jerusalem or Samaria.

We choose the mountain or the temple.

We choose white or black.

We choose young or old.

We choose traditional or contemporary.

Either category we pick is inevitably wrong because it is man-centered rather than God-centered.

Jesus said to the woman,

> "Woman, believe me, the hour is coming when neither on this mountain nor in Jerusalem will you worship the Father. You worship what you do not know; we worship what we know, for salvation is from the Jews. But the hour is coming, and is now here, when the true worshipers will worship the Father in spirit and truth, for the Father is seeking such people to worship him. God is spirit, and those who worship him must worship in spirit and truth." (John 4:21–24)

Jesus' answer was actually a nonanswer. Her question was about the mountain or the temple. Jesus' answer was about spirit and truth. The Lord wanted this woman to understand that it is not about the place, time, or style of worship. It is about the essence of worship. Worship is about God and not about us. When we recognize this essential truth, the worship of the church will not be divided by color lines.

WORSHIP IS FOR AND ABOUT GOD

Biblical worship is not color-based. Ultimately, there is no such thing as black worship, white worship, or any other color of worship. Worship is both *for* God and *about* God. True worship is God-centered, not race-driven.

At the same time, true worship is not colorblind. A person who claims to be colorblind typically means that he or she does not discriminate against others based on race. That's a good thing. Yet the term can also carry negative connotations. Racism in America has historically been public, systemic, and institutional. It is now more covert and less prevalent, though no less real. Colorblindness may be a failure or refusal to see the subtle but real racial discrimination that happens around you. This is easy to do whenever you are in a setting where most of the people look like you. The only way to avoid the errors of color-based or color-blind worship is to make sure you put God before culture. When God the Father, God the Son, and God the Holy Spirit is the infinite center of worship, it invariably transcends color, culture, and comfort.

Ethnic harmony in the church is a lofty goal. The divided world desperately needs the church to be the church. What steps can we take to show the world the difference Christ makes? Permit me to offer a simple but strategic step. First, let me give a little background.

In 2014, our church in Jacksonville merged with another congregation in our city. A more than one-hundred-year-old predominantly black congregation married a more than one-hundred-year-old predominantly white congregation.

As this merger took place, racial strife consumed our city and country. The news of our new work was considered a light in dark times. We started fast. And, by God's grace, we are still going strong. Sure, there have been bumps along the way. But the Lord has been faithful to us.

As a result of our story, I am often asked about matters of the church and race. I'm glad to be whatever help I can. But I am no expert on these matters. God deserves all the glory. And whatever human credit is deserved should go to the good and godly people I serve, not any stellar leadership on my part. I have taken steps of faith with fear and trembling. God has honored those steps of faith to the praise of His glory.

MOVING TOGETHER IN WORSHIP

There is, however, a bit of advice I am eager to share about racial harmony in the local church. It is no grand scheme. It is the direct opposite. I recommend that pastors and churches take small steps toward racial harmony. Big steps are generally preferred over small steps. But I contend that it was the little steps forward we took over time that enabled us to take grand leaps down the road.

Here's my advice: to pursue racial diversity and unity in a local church, lead in such a way that biblical elements of worship are not associated with one cultural tradition. Force corporate worship to transcend cultural preferences. Don't let your people think your way is the only way.

As you select music for your worship services, pick good music that crosses color lines. Your church should sing biblically sound, gospel-saturated, Christ-exalting music. That should be non-negotiable. But work to introduce your people to music for worship from unexpected sources. Let them appreciate the music. Then let them find out where it came from. Of course, I am not suggesting that you select theologically questionable music. I am suggesting that you reach outside your cultural tribe and find good music you can commend. You can also apply this principle to the speakers you invite, books you use, and resources you recommend in your church.

Throughout the year, I invite pastors to fill the pulpit for me. Early on, I asked several white brothers I know to preach for us. And at some point, my congregation began to associate good preaching with good preaching, not color. We also took some Contemporary Christian music, put some "seasoning salt" on it, and used it in our services. These songs became meaningful parts of our services, even though they were not from expected sources. No, changes in our congregation's thinking and attitude did not happen overnight. But they did happen over time. (Incidentally, significant change always takes time. It is not wise to initiate substantial change in the church if you do not intend to stay to see it through.)

Our church has taken big steps of faith in seeking to worship beyond color lines. Dramatic headlines grab attention. Unfortunately, the underlying story details are often ignored. We were able to take some giant leaps because we took many small steps of faith. It will not be easy. But it will be worth it. The psalmist was right: "Behold, how good and pleasant it is when brothers dwell in unity!" (Ps. 133:1).

Chapter 23

> > > ✝ < < <

TWO TYPES OF GOD-TALK

A church in my hometown hosted an annual twenty-four-hour preaching marathon. Yep. You read that right. Twenty-four hours of preaching. From Saturday evening to Sunday evening, a sermon was preached at the top of every hour, with joyful singing in between. You could scarcely find a seat in the building the whole time.

My young preacher friends and I would block off this weekend. Outside of a need for burgers, we were there to hear every message—our local church activities excluded, of course. As we grew older and life commitments changed, we could no longer pull the long haul.

One night, however, I ventured out alone to hear the "Midnight Special"—the prime preaching spot at midnight on Saturday night of the marathon. It was always the most well-attended hour. One of the city's favorite preachers spoke that night. He was often given this prime preaching spot. For some reason, I was called up to the pulpit before the message. I had the best seat in the house.

The preacher called Psalm 23 as his sermon text. You could sense the anticipation and curiosity. A good chunk of the congregation quoted it aloud as the preacher read it. What could he say new about this beloved passage? Well, the preacher did not say anything

new about this well-known and much-beloved psalm. He did say
something different about it. Instead of preaching what David said
in Psalm 23, he talked about *how* David said it. He argued that there
are two types of God-talk in Psalm 23.

First, David talked *about* God: "The LORD is my shepherd; I
shall not want. He makes me lie down in green pastures. He leads
me beside still waters. He restores my soul. He leads me in paths of
righteousness for his name's sake" (Ps. 23:1–3).

In the middle of the psalm, David shifts from talking about
God to talking *to* God: "Even though I walk through the valley of
the shadow of death, I will fear no evil, for you are with me; your
rod and your staff, they comfort me. You prepare a table before me
in the presence of my enemies; you anoint my head with oil; my cup
overflows" (Ps. 23:4–5).

The final verse of the psalm again shifts to talking about the
Lord: "Surely goodness and mercy shall follow me all the days of
my life, and I shall dwell in the house of the LORD forever" (Ps. 23:6).

The congregation did not take this sermon well. They expected
the preacher to draw fresh water from this old well. But this novel
reading of Psalm 23 was too much. The congregation sat quietly
through the entire sermon. In a traditional black-church setting,
that was not a good thing. This preacher was chosen for this service
because his dynamic preaching could warm up the coldest congregation. Not on this night. But I assure you that the congregation's
disinterest was no reflection on the sermon. The message ministered to me and is still one of the best sermons I have ever heard.

TO GOD AND ABOUT GOD

I often think about this late-night sermon when I read or
hear Psalm 23. It has become a key to how I unlock the psalms

devotionally. As I read psalms, I instinctively ask if the psalmist is talking *to* God or *about* God. The consideration of this prayerful and worshipful God-talk also runs through my mind in corporate worship. As I sing with other believers, I find myself asking if the songs are to God or about God.

Unfortunately, many contemporary worship songs are neither to God nor about God. They are songs written with a message to comfort, encourage, or motivate the hearer, but God is conspicuously absent from the message of the songs. Or He is only there as a prop for the man-centered message of the songs.

Don't get me wrong. There is a place for this kind of special music in worship. After all, Scripture instructs us to sing psalms, hymns, and spiritual songs to one another (Eph. 5:19; Col. 3:16). But our worship should not be dominated by songs to or about the worshipers. God-talk, not self-talk, should characterize our singing.

There is a genre of music called "Inspiration." Its goal is to do what the term suggests—to inspire the listener. The music we sing in worship should inspire the congregation. But it should not be our primary aim to be inspirational. Edification of the saints, not the inspiration of an audience, should drive worship leaders (1 Cor. 14:26).

Sin, sorrow, sickness, suffering, and other struggles burden Christians. Members drag themselves to church on Sunday mornings, seeking hope to enable them to fight the good fight another week. Another day. An uplifting service can strengthen the saints to persevere in the faith. But wise spiritual leaders should ask, "Who are we uplifting?" Is the service designed to exalt the worthy name of the Lord? Or is the goal to boost the sagging morale of attendees?

Self-help music may be motivational. It is not worship. Whatever it means to worship God in spirit and truth, it at least means this: worship is not about us! Paul identified the "target audience" of Christian worship: "For from him and through him and to him are all things. To him be glory forever. Amen" (Rom. 11:36). God is the subject and object of worship.[9] It is for God. And it is about God.

What about the needs, hurts, and trials of the gathered saints? This question betrays a faulty understanding of God's glory, people's needs, and true worship. God is what people need! Not our profound sermons. Not our sensational music. Not our creative elements. Ultimately, essentially, and desperately, people need God. The worship of God and the meeting of needs are not separate issues. And they are not in opposition to each other. Paul assured, "And my God will supply every need of yours according to his riches in glory in Christ Jesus. To our God and Father be glory forever and ever" (Phil. 4:19–20).

POINTING PEOPLE TO GOD

The way to meet the deep needs of the soul in worship is to point people to God, then get out of the way. Every element of the worship service should point to Jesus, not just the sermon. People need to see Him, not us.

When worship music is criticized for being too personal or even too "romantic," Psalm 23 comes to my mind. David sings in the most intimate terms.

"The LORD is *my* shepherd."

"He makes *me* lie down in green pastures."

"He restores *my* soul."

"You are with *me*."

"You prepare a table before *me* in the presence of *my* enemies."

"*I* shall dwell in the house of the LORD forever."

We do not know the historical background of Psalm 23. David

may have composed this song as a young shepherd or a wise old man. He may have penned these words during tranquil moments of meditation or a difficult season of persecution. No one knows. But what we do not know about the background of this psalm does not hinder our ability to understand or appreciate it in any way. Believers around the world and throughout the centuries relate to Psalm 23, as David seems to say, "Whatever my circumstances, because the Lord is my shepherd, I shall not want."

Psalm 23 is a song of confident trust in the Lord that ministers to God's people in various seasons of life. Yet it is not about David. It is about the Lord. It is not about the helpless sheep. It is about the good Shepherd. It is not about the needy guest. It is about the gracious Host.

Psalm 23 ministers to people without singing to or about people. David ministers to us by singing to and about the Lord. This is what God's people need on Sunday morning. The service cannot help them if it is about them. Sheep need a shepherd. Preach and sing to exalt the Good Shepherd, who laid down His life for the sheep (John 10:11).

Chapter 24

WORSHIP AND GOD'S KINGDOM

What is the relationship between church and politics? Should the church stay as far away from politics as it can? Or should the church be actively involved in politics? If so, to what degree should the church be politically engaged?

There is no consensus on the answers to these questions. Christians are unable to reach agreement because the questions are somewhat misguided. The questions assume that political involvement is optional. That is not so. Politics are inevitable. Every sphere of life is touched by political agendas, one way or the other.

For decades, the word *evangelical* has been used to identify Bible-believing and gospel-driven Christians. It is now associated by the world with right-wing politics. Meanwhile, near election time, many black churches give their pulpits to left-wing politicians who preach a gospel of this world and not of our true King. This is the wrong kind of church politics. We are first citizens of another kingdom, with primary allegiance to the King of kings.

Ancient Philippi was a Roman colony. Residents of Philippi were citizens of Rome. And the Philippians were very proud of that fact. Paul reminded the Philippian Christians that they owed their highest devotion to an infinitely greater authority: "But our citizenship is in heaven, and from it we await a Savior, the Lord Jesus Christ, who will transform our lowly body to be like his glorious body, by the power that enables him even to subject all things to himself" (Phil. 3:20–21).

We worship heaven's King.

We seek heaven's pleasure.

We pursue heaven's agenda.

We declare heaven's message.

We submit to heaven's authority.

Christians are to be political in the original sense of the word, *polis*. A polis was a city-state in ancient Greece. The term could also refer to the city center or the body of citizens that made up the city. The church is political in that the church itself is a polis. Our "patriotism" should be to the heavenly kingdom. Facing growing hostility from the Roman culture, Peter told troubled churches, "But you are a chosen race, a royal priesthood, a holy nation, a people for his own possession" (1 Peter 2:9).

A HOLY NATION

To most of us, the word *nation* signifies government, geography, and citizenship. As a result, we do not think of the church as a nation. But that's what the church is. However, the church is not like the nations of the world. We are a "holy nation," set apart to and for God.

Christians are not primarily called to engage in partisan politics. In the United States, we are blessed to be citizens of a country where we can and should participate in the processes of government. But kingdom politics is our primary calling. What does that look like? As God's special people, we are to "proclaim the excellencies of him who called you out of darkness into his marvelous light" (1 Peter 2:9).

The church proclaims the excellencies of God in worship. It is essential that the church gathers for worship (Heb. 10:24–25). Worship is not a community event. It is a Christian event. The "worship wars" of past decades argued about whether worship services were for the saved or unsaved. Ultimately, both sides were wrong. The purpose of worship governs the practice of worship. The purpose of worship is to proclaim the excellencies of God. True worship is God-centered. We do not gather for worship to support our cause, relieve our problems, or entertain our preferences. We worship to exalt the Lord, who is worthy to be praised.

We also proclaim the excellencies of God in witness. We proclaim God's excellencies to one another when we gather for worship. The audience may be different. But the message is the same. We proclaim God's excellencies to the world when we scatter from worship. "Our praises to God bear witness to the world," commented Edmund Clowney. "The heart of evangelism is doxological."[10] Psalm 96:3–4 says, "Declare his glory among the nations, his marvelous works among all the peoples! For great is the Lord, and greatly to be praised; he is to be feared above all gods."

I am sure there are members of my congregation (and some people outside of my congregation) who do not like that I do not speak out on political issues of the day. In reality, I talk about political matters all the time in my sermons. I just don't talk about them in the manner that they want. I try to stubbornly address cultural issues as a Christian preacher, not a political pundit.

HOLY ENGAGEMENT IN OUR EARTHLY SPHERE

It is not my position that the church should only focus on spiritual, heavenly, eternal things. To withdraw from the world around us is to rebel against the call of Christ to be salt and light (Matt. 5:13–16). We must engage the world around us. But we must show up as the church. To worship the donkey or elephant is idolatry. We join heaven in singing, "Worthy is the Lamb who was slain, to receive power and wealth and wisdom and might and honor and glory and blessing!" (Rev. 5:12).

Many issues plague our society and I am deeply passionate about them. But none of the political parties' platforms represent the kingdom of God on these issues. Their focus is on earthly kingdoms. And too often, they either sin against the biblical commands of God by omission or commission. If you embrace a biblical worldview, you inevitably vote against candidates, just as much as you vote for them. No candidate, piece of legislation, or Supreme Court decision will usher in the kingdom of God. This does not mean that we should not try to make this world a better place. It means that we must recognize that the United States of America (or whatever country you live in) is not the kingdom of heaven. Read the following two sentences slowly and carefully. Let the world be the world. Let the church be the church.

Perhaps the church does not rally, march, protest, boycott, sit in, lobby, or cancel. But if you are doing church right, your congregation is passionately involved in the business of the nation of God. Christianity is political. The church is in the business of revolution. The gospel is kingdom propaganda. Baptism is civil disobedience. Worship is a peaceful protest. Preaching is counterintelligence. Prayer is subversive activity.

That's real church politics. We proclaim Jesus Christ is Lord, no matter who is in the White House, the state capitol, or city hall. We demand every person who joins us to declare allegiance to Christ by the public humiliation of water baptism. We come together to have bread and wine in remembrance of the body and blood of Christ. We believe that what we share in Christ is greater than whatever differences we have. We give when we lose our jobs. We sing although our families are in trouble. We pray for healing when we get sick. We forgive when we are wronged. We come to church on Sundays, rather than going to the beach.

In the invocation of the Lord's Prayer, we pray as children who trust the provision and protection of our heavenly Father: "Our Father in heaven" (Matt. 6:9). In the first petition, we pray as worshipers with wet eyes, covered mouths, broken hearts, captivated minds, and bent knees before the holy presence of God: "Hallowed be your name."

Then, in the second petition, we pray as lobbyists dissatisfied with the present order of things, appealing to God to make things right in the world: "Your kingdom come." This is the shortest petition in the Model Prayer. Yet it is the biggest petition you can pray. To sincerely pray, "Your kingdom come," is to acknowledge, confess, and denounce your treasonous loyalties. For God's kingdom to come, our little kingdoms must go.

Whose side are you on?

Chapter 25

✝

➤ ➤ ➤ ◄ ◄ ◄

YOUTH ARE NOT THE CHURCH OF TOMORROW

I was a boy preacher who started pastoring my first church at the age of seventeen. That was more than thirty years ago. However, the most common question I get (beyond what does H.B. stand for) is, what was it like to pastor at seventeen?

I admit that I was not ready to pastor a church as a senior in high school. But I was more prepared than you would think. My father and the men around him poured much into me. And the congregation I grew up in was committed to investing in its young people. It was not a large church. We did not have a full-time youth pastor, designated youth facilities, or a large ministry budget. But the membership cared about the children and youth. They believed in us.

If you were to hear a recording of one of my father's Sunday sermons, you would hear congregational amens and crying babies in the background. We did not have a nursery for parents to drop off their children. Little children sat in "big church" with their parents. And to be honest, I don't think that was a bad thing. I am a living witness that children can sit quietly, listen attentively, and respond sincerely to the Word of God and the gospel of Christ.

When babies became too restless in the service, a frustrated mother would get up to take the baby out. My dad would stop preaching and tell the mother to sit down. "That baby is not bothering me," he would say. "I only get upset when some of these older ones who should know better start acting up."

Once a month was youth Sunday, in which the young people took over the service. The children's choir (called "The Tender Voices") and youth choir sang. Youth were also selected to read the Scripture, offer the prayer, and give the announcements. Then one of the young preacher boys was given a chance to preach. Looking back, I am blown away by how generous my father was in sharing his pulpit with young men learning to preach.

The congregation did not just patiently endure these Sundays. They encouraged us to give our lives to the service of the Lord. It was not that the church gave us a chance to participate once a month and then sent us away for the rest of the month. On the first Sunday, the youth sang in the mass choir, and the junior deacons helped serve Communion. On the third Sunday, the kids ushered. Every week, some place was carved into the service to give the opportunity to participate in the worship services.

Occasionally, a member would complain about youth Sunday, when the children's choir would sing and the youth would usher. And they would threaten to stay home or go visiting when the young people led the church. My father responded to these complaints from the pulpit. He explained why ministry to and by the children was significant. These speeches ended with my father saying, "Remember, Sinai, the youth are not the church of tomorrow. They are the church of today. If we do not invest in the young people today, there will not be a church tomorrow." This became a refrain that many church members repeated over the years.

Is this the sentiment of your church?

BRINGING OUR CHILDREN TO JESUS

Have you exiled the young people from the worship life of the church? Have you put the children in a nursery so the adults can worship in peace and quiet? Have you developed a separate youth culture so that when it is time for them to transition into adult services, they do not feel at home? Are you failing to identify and invest in young people whom the Lord is calling into ministry because they are isolated from the body-life of the church?

Some pastors advocate for a family-based ministry that abolishes all age-graded ministry programs in the church. That is not my position. But I do believe we should consider the unintentional damage we may be doing to the church by segregating the generations of the congregation. This is not how Scripture envisions corporate worship.

The fifth word of the Decalogue commands, "Honor your father and your mother, that your days may be long in the land that the LORD your God is giving you" (Ex. 20:12). This was not the "children's sermon" of the Ten Commandments. It was God's message to all the children of Israel—young and old.

In Ephesians and Colossians, Paul gave instructions to the children (Eph. 6:1–3; Col. 3:20). These were not messages given in the children's Sunday school class or weeklong vacation Bible school. For that matter, the instructions to fathers were not given in the men's ministry and the instructions to husbands and wives were not given at the married couples' retreat. These letters were read in the public assemblies of these local churches. The children were a part of these meetings and heard what the apostle wrote to them, along with what he wrote to their fathers.

In my father's church, parents made their children participate in church activities. Many of my generation said, "When I have children, I am not going to make them go to church and be involved." This was foolish thinking and a tragic mistake. The wisdom of God is the direct opposite: "Train up a child in the way he should go; even when he is old he will not depart from it" (Prov. 22:6). This proverb does not mean that if you give your children spiritual training, they will never go wrong. The principle is that we should point our children in the right direction when they are young, if we expect them to travel the right path when they are no longer under our authority and influence.

THE BATTLE AGAINST OUR CHILDREN

The flesh, the world, and the devil do not give our young people time and space to make up their own minds about spiritual matters. The enemy aggressively pursues our children. Moses gave Pharaoh the word of the Lord, "Let my people go free to worship me" (see, e.g., Ex. 5:1; 7:16; 8:1). The hard-hearted Pharaoh initially refused, asking, "Who is the Lord?" He later changed his mind slightly. He would permit the men of Israel to go into the wilderness to worship their God. But they had to leave their children behind (Ex. 10:7–11).

Is this not the satanic mindset of our God-hating culture? Society has disregarded the convictions of the faithful. But it is going after our children. If you do not reach children when they are young, it will be much harder to do so later. The church does not seem to believe this. And we sit back wondering why so many of the young people have disappeared from the church. All the while, the desires of the flesh, the desires of the eyes, and the pride of possessions consume our young people (1 John 2:15–17).

The first line of defense against the enemy is the home. God-fearing parents raising their children in the instruction and admonition of the Lord (Eph. 6:4) can change our society. The church cannot replace the role of parents in raising godly children. It must not try. But the church should provide "air cover" for Christian parents fighting the good fight for their children.

When some parents tried to bring their children to Jesus, the disciples turned them away. Jesus rebuked them—the disciples, not the parents. "Let the little children come to me and do not hinder them," Jesus said, "for to such belongs the kingdom of heaven" (Matt. 19:14). Youth are not the church of tomorrow. They are the church of today. Shape the worship life of your church so that the young people may grow as Jesus grew (Luke 2:52).

Chapter 26

✝

HAVE YOU BEEN WITH JESUS?

A friend and I talked about a conference we had both attended, during different years. As he listed the speakers he heard, I asked about a particular name he mentioned. I knew of this man's ministry but had never heard him speak. I inquired, "Can he preach?"

My friend answered affirmatively and emphatically. "He knows how to handle the text," my friend expanded. "And you can tell he's been with Jesus."

The conversation ended there because I did not say anything else. I could not say anything else. I was stuck on the statement, "And you can tell he's been with Jesus."

The language of the statement was not new to me. I recognized the biblical reference.

Peter and John were arrested after healing a crippled man in the name of Jesus. The authorities threatened the apostles not to speak in the name of Jesus anymore. Yet the apostles did not waver in their Christian witness, as they stood before the Jewish rulers, elders and scribes. "This Jesus is the stone that was rejected by you, the builders, which has become the cornerstone," Peter defiantly proclaimed. "And there is salvation in no one else, for there is no other name under heaven given among men by which we must be saved" (Acts 4:11–12).

Then, almost parenthetically, Luke noted, "Now when they saw the boldness of Peter and John, and perceived that they were uneducated, common men, they were astonished. And they recognized that they had been with Jesus" (Acts 4:13).

The apostles did not have formal education, institutional clout, or ministerial prominence. They did not have any ministerial credentials that would have caused the Jewish religious leaders to consider them credible. For that matter, they could not claim any ministerial credentials we would deem acceptable or admirable today. But it is evident that these ordinary men had been with the Lord Jesus Christ.

This observation was no compliment. The religious leaders were not commending Peter and John's Christlikeness. The statement about Jesus was an indictment against the apostles. The religious establishment was made up of the builders who rejected the cornerstone (Acts 4:11). They knew what kind of man Jesus was and what type of ministry He had, even though they did not believe in Him.

UNDENIABLE

The miracle Peter and John performed could not be denied. The man who lay by the gate of the temple had been crippled all his life. Then, all of a sudden, he was running about the temple complex, praising God. The apostles claimed the man was healed in the name of the crucified but risen Savior, the Lord Jesus. The religious leaders could not deny this. So they commanded Peter and John to stop speaking of Jesus and threatened dire consequences. Yet the former fishermen had seen and heard too much to be silent.

Taking all of this in, these unbelieving religionists could only come to one logical conclusion. These men had been with Jesus. It was a plain statement of fact, even though the religious leaders did not know the magnitude of what they said. They were talking better than they understood. The words and deeds of the apostles made it obvious that they had spent time with Jesus of Nazareth.

This is how all pastor-teachers, worship leaders, and servant-leaders in the church should be described. Whether you minister in an up-front role or serve behind the scenes, it should be obvious that you have been with Jesus. This is also the way every true Christian should be described. Charles Spurgeon wrote, "Oh! My brethren, it were well if this condemnation, so forced from the lips of enemies, could also be compelled by our own example."[11] Unfortunately, until my friend's passing statement, I had never heard anyone described that way.

> **Whether you minister in an up-front role or serve behind the scenes, it should be obvious that you have been with Jesus.**

After scanning my mental files, I double-clicked on my own ministry. When I stand to preach, is it obvious to those who hear me that I have been with Jesus?

I take pride in the fact that I do not go to the pulpit unprepared. I firmly believe a passion to preach without a discipline to prepare is just a desire to perform. I desperately desire to be "a worker who has no need to be ashamed, rightly dividing the word of truth" (2 Tim. 2:15). But the truth is that you can go to the pulpit with a well-prepared sermon, without any evidence ever giving the sense that you have been with Jesus.

Whatever we do for the Lord should be done with excellence. By this, I do not mean what the deacons in my father's church would call "an outside show to an unfriendly world." I simply mean that whatever bears God's name deserves our best. We should be like the woman who offered costly worship to Jesus (Mark 14:3). We are often instead like those who indignantly asked, "Why was the ointment wasted like that?" (Mark 14:4).

The Lord deserves the best we can offer Him. But we have missed the point if we only offer Him our gifts, talents, and service, and not ourselves. The Lord wants you, not just your preaching skill, musical ability, technical savvy, organizational skills, or charismatic personality. God wants your heart. When your heart is His, there will be something different about the ministry you offer. Something you cannot take credit for. Something you cannot explain. It will be obvious that you have been with Jesus.

COMING OR GOING

Many mornings, when my family wakes up, I am in shorts and a T-shirt for my walk. Some mornings I am heading out; other mornings, I am just getting in. But they know whether I am coming or going without me telling them. They can smell the difference. If I am heading out, I get hugs. If I am returning, I get orders to take a shower!

The congregation can also tell if those of us who lead worship are coming or going. Paul wrote, "For we are the aroma of Christ to God among those who are being saved and among those who are perishing, to one a fragrance from death to death, to the other a fragrance from life to life" (2 Cor. 2:15–16). To have the aroma of Christ in your life and ministry, you must spend time with Jesus. Our public ministry should be the overflow of private devotion. This is the difference between being with Jesus and merely being around Jesus.

Do you have a daily quiet time?

Do you read God's Word to feed your soul?

Do you spend meaningful time in prayer?

Private time with the Lord should precede public time for the Lord. The more you submit to Christ in humility, the more you can stand for Christ with boldness. The religious leaders were amazed by the boldness of Peter and John. There was no fear of man in them. Being with Jesus will produce in you a holy boldness to exalt the Lord in all circumstances. You need this boldness, not just when you face enemies of Christ, but also as you lead your fellow followers of Christ in worship.

Do you have clean hands of irreproachable integrity?

Do you have steady feet that walk in obedience?

Do you have dirty knees from time spend in prayer?

Do you have weary eyes from diligent preparation?

Do you have a renewed mind of biblical conviction?

Do you have a broken heart for lost people?

Do you have a listening ear for spiritual direction?

Do you have strong arms from bearing others' burdens?

Do you have a faithful tongue that speaks the truth in love?

Do you have firm legs that stand strong in spiritual boldness?

Have you been with Jesus?

Chapter 27

✝

YOU ARE NOT THE STORY

I am a news junkie. To be more accurate, I used to be a news junkie. My wife and I often watched cable news together. We skipped around to all of the cable news stations. While we did other things, the news played in the background. However, I now find it painfully difficult to watch the news.

One issue drove my withdrawal from watching the news: It seems the news no longer reports the news. When you turn on the news, the same thing happens virtually every time. The anchors or hosts announce a new item. These days, almost every story is "Breaking News." A brief overview is given of the news report, with a strategically edited clip or graphic that points to a conclusion.

Then a panel of experts discusses what we just heard or did not hear. The panelists are clearly partisans who promote their agenda or affiliation no matter what. The discussions regularly turn into arguments, with multiple people yelling at the same time. It's a mess!

Initially, this did not dampen my passion for the news. I just decided it might be better to read the news sites rather than watching the news shows. Nope. That was no better. The twenty-four-hour news apps and websites are basically promotional sites for anchors and reporters on the news shows.

And here is what finally turned me off. As you scroll the news channel websites, instead of the news, you'll find clips of the latest rant by someone who was supposed to be reporting the news. The featured video is not about what the government official said or did, for instance. It is a "hot take" of what the reporter said to or about the government official.

Forgive me for venting. But I really can't take it anymore. I wish we could go back to a time when journalists reported the news rather than trying to make news. No, I am not nostalgic about a time that did not exist, when the networks reported the news objectively. But there was a time when news people presented themselves as objective and tried to be. The new reality is another symptom of the divided culture we now live in.

But something else is at play here. Reports are not just responding to cultural divisions; they are feeding into them. Because too many news people want to break news (almost at any cost), we no longer learn what's going on in our communities, nation, and the world by watching the news. It may be making us dumb. After watching a few minutes of a news telecast, I find myself turning the channel in frustration, grumbling to the reporter on the screen, "You are not the story!"

IT'S ALL ABOUT JESUS

After pointing the finger at news reports, I need to consider the remaining fingers pointing back at those of us who lead worship.

We who stand in the pulpit need this reminder just as much as those who sit at the news desk. Christian ministers are charged to preach the Word (2 Tim. 4:1–2). The Lord commands it. The truth demands it. The hearers need it. Yet this is always the danger of inserting so much of ourselves into the sermon, by our content or delivery, that the message is obscured. People should not leave the sermon learning more about the preacher than Christ. When we stand to preach the Word, we should prayerfully whisper to ourselves, "You are not the story."

The term *minister* is used often these days to describe those who serve, which is a good thing. It is usually applied to the church members rather than worship leaders. But we are also ministers. We are ministers of the Word (Acts 6:4). As heralds, it is our sacred duty to proclaim the message of the King. It is not our message. We do not have editorial authority over the message we proclaim. And the message is not about us.

The relevant question is not, "Can he preach?" It is, "What does he preach?" Paul said, "For what we proclaim is not ourselves, but Jesus Christ as Lord, with ourselves as your servants for Jesus' sake" (2 Cor. 4:5). We must resist the temptation to make the preaching moment about us, at all costs. The sermon is not a time to display our giftedness. It is the time to exalt the grace and truth of the Lord Jesus Christ.

Those who lead the congregation in musical praise need the same rebuke. Your gifts and talents are an asset to the worship life of the church. To be honest, I do not think we pastors say that enough. The loving labor of those who play instruments and lead singing is a tremendous blessing to our churches. But the worship service is not a "set" for you to put on a show. In a real sense, your task is similar to the preacher's role. In music or preaching, we are to point the congregation to the Lord Jesus Christ. Then get out of the way! Let Christ be the center of attention. And do not photobomb the Lord by trying to make it about you.

THE WHOLE SERVICE IS ABOUT JESUS

I have not addressed creative elements of worship services in this book. For sure, this is a matter that deserves careful discussion. That discussion should best take place among the leaders of the local church, but permit me to say here the principle I give to preachers and musicians applies to other creative artists in our churches: You are not the story!

When I was a young pastor, two young women started attending our church. After some weeks, they joined. I was so encouraged. It was my experience that if prospects kicked the tires for a while before joining, they were more likely to stick around. After joining, the young ladies asked to speak with me about getting involved. Way cool! They wanted to join our praise dancers team. I informed them that we did not have one. And I never saw them again. This incident is a warning. Your art is not more important than the church.

Paul confronted the Corinthians about putting their gifts ahead of the good of others: "What then, brothers? When you come together, each one has a hymn, a lesson, a revelation, a tongue, or an interpretation. Let all things be done for building up" (1 Cor. 14:26).

You are not a news anchor, on-scene reporter, or expert panelist. You are a Christian minister and messenger.

The worship service is not an opportunity to put our gifts, talents, and artistry on display. We are to build up the saints in faith, devotion, and reverence for Christ.

Some Greeks made the long journey and joined the crowds of worshipers in Jerusalem for one of the annual Jewish feasts. They approached Philip, whom they rightly assumed was a follower of Christ. Then they made the request that caused them to travel to the holy city: "Sir, we wish to see Jesus" (John 12:21). These words are on a plaque posted on my pulpit. It is a needed weekly reminder that I am not the story. People have come to see Jesus, not meet me.

This is the desperate request of every person we lead in worship, whether they recognize it or not. They want to see Jesus. Believers and unbelievers need news from another network in glory. Give them gospel truth, not fake news. "Him we proclaim," Paul testifies, "warning everyone and teaching everyone with all wisdom, that we may present everyone mature in Christ" (Col. 1:28). You are not a news anchor, on-scene reporter, or expert panelist. You are a Christian minister and messenger. Present the good news of Jesus Christ faithfully and clearly every time you stand before the worshiping congregation. And stay out of the news! You are not the story.

Chapter 28

✝

DON'T ASSUME ANYTHING

Y̲ou remember the three Hebrews boys in the fiery furnace . . ."

"You remember when Jesus stilled the storm on the Sea of Galilee . . ."

"You remember what Paul said about justification by faith alone . . ."

My sermons were filled with statements like these as a young pastor. I took for granted that the congregation knew and understood these passing references. Assuming shared knowledge and convictions, I often skipped over the explanation of biblical texts and themes and I rushed to get to the point I wanted to make.

That all changed after a conversation with a member I considered one of the more spiritually mature young adults in our church. I had to hide my surprise when she said to me, "You know, Pastor, when you say, 'You remember . . .' in your sermons, I want to stand up and say, 'No, I don't.' I don't know many of the Bible stories you mention. But I am learning a lot from your preaching."

She meant these statements as a compliment. But they hit me like a ton of bricks. If she could not follow along, how many more of my members struggled with the same thing? As a result of this eye-opening conversation, I determined not to assume anything in the pulpit.

Everyone who leads the church in worship should practice this principle: don't assume anything.

Paul began his ministry by proclaiming the risen Savior in Jewish synagogues. He reasoned with unbelieving Jews through the Scriptures, showing them how the Lord Jesus Christ fulfilled messianic prophecy. When Paul became the apostle to the Gentiles, he adopted a different approach. On Mars Hill (Acts 17), he reasoned with the religiously superstitious Athenians, who sought to appease many gods. They did not share the monotheistic convictions of the Israelites. Paul started with creation and walked them forward to the resurrection of Jesus. He even quoted their philosophers to gain common ground with his hearers.

Leading worship in the average church today is like being in the Areopagus in Athens rather than the temple in Jerusalem. Don't assume anything. For God's sake, don't assume where people stand as it relates to the gospel of Jesus Christ. This is a common mistake church leaders often make. We believe the gospel and want to make it known. We assume that the gospel is foundational for our people. And we build on that foundation that may not exist in the hearts and minds of those who attend. We must make sure the foundation is set and settled before we start building on it.

Leading worship in the average church today is like being in the Areopagus in Athens rather than the temple in Jerusalem.

I have a friend who presents the gospel in every message he preaches. This is not uncommon. At least, it should not be. We should give a brief gospel presentation in every sermon. But what makes my friend's preaching stand out is how intentionally and excellently he does it. I have heard him preach in many pastors' conferences. Yet in a room full of pastors, he explains the gospel and calls for a response. This is how we should lead worship every week in our local churches. Don't assume the gospel. Make the gospel explicit.

In your sermons each week plead with your hearers to run to the cross. Sing songs that proclaim the Word of God and the testimony of Jesus Christ. Read through the metanarrative of Scriptures from the Old and New Testaments. Pray for open doors for the gospel and the salvation of the lost in your circle of contact and throughout the nations. Show your people the gospel by practicing baptism and the Lord's Supper in meaningful ways. Don't assume anything.

I do not say this to be condescending. I say this with a heavy sense of pastoral concern. The biblical message is not simply what your people already think. The New Testament calls the gospel a mystery. It is the truth that is not known until God reveals it. Nothing in the world prepares you for the gospel but the gospel. In every way, the world opposes gospel truth.

We meet for weekly worship because we need to have our minds renewed by the truth that we will not hear anywhere else. Use the time your church meets together for worship strategically. Do not take anything for granted. Do not leave the spiritual formation of your people to chance. Do not assume what the members of the congregation know, understand, or believe.

DO NOT ASSUME WHAT
THE CONGREGATION KNOWS

We live in a day of rampant biblical illiteracy. Many people, including regular churchgoers, may not know the major characters, classic stories, or fundamental doctrines of the Bible. They may not know the great hymns and beloved songs of the church. They may not know the meaning or significance of special days in the Christian calendar.

Don't complain about this reality. Don't shout at the darkness, blaming the cultural drift away from Judeo-Christian values. Don't bemoan the demise of Sunday school or Bible study. View the problem of biblical illiteracy as an opportunity to introduce your people to the Bible, teach them the Scriptures, and shape their Christian worldview. Help your people to "grow in the grace and knowledge of our Lord and Savior Jesus Christ" (2 Peter 3:18).

DO NOT ASSUME WHAT
THE CONGREGATION UNDERSTANDS

This principle is a step forward from the previous one. People may know the passage you reference. That does not mean they understand the meaning of it. They may know that certain things happen in your worship services. That does not mean they understand why these things happen. They may know that there are certain beliefs your congregation does not embrace. That does not mean they understand the convictions that force you to refrain from activities the church down the street practices.

We do not know who wrote Psalm 119. It is a long, intricate, beautiful ode to the sufficiency of Scripture in every season of life. Whoever penned this great psalm evidently knew and believed the Word of God. Yet, throughout the psalm, he regularly prays, "Give me understanding." This oft-repeated petition confesses that we cannot understand divine truth with our finite minds.

"The natural person does not accept the things of the Spirit of God," wrote Paul, "for they are folly to him, and he is not able to understand them because they are spiritually discerned" (1 Cor. 2:14). Familiarity with the wording of a text does not guarantee spiritual illumination. Dig deep in your preparation to help your people see beyond a superficial understanding of the text.

DO NOT ASSUME WHAT
THE CONGREGATION BELIEVES

A person can know a biblical text, truth, or theme. That person can also understand the God-intended meaning of it. But you should not assume that knowledge and understanding translate into faith. Many congregants have been squeezed into the world's false value system (Rom. 12:2). Their theological, ethical, and moral views have been shaped by popular culture rather than biblical truth. Make the gospel explicit. Preach expositionally and apologetically. Do not assume what members of the congregation believe.

Jesus said, "If you abide in my word, you are truly my disciples, and you will know the truth, and the truth will set you free" (John 8:31–32). These are famous words of Jesus. However, many do not recognize this statement was made to Jews who had believed Him (John 8:31a). Stated faith is not necessarily saving faith. There is a difference between the profession of faith and the possession of faith. You must believe what you believe. We must help professing believers continue in the Word that they may know the truth and be spiritually free. Peter exhorted, "In your hearts honor Christ the Lord as holy, always being prepared to make a defense to anyone who asks you for a reason for the hope that is in you" (1 Peter 3:15).

Chapter 29

THREE PETITIONS FOR WORSHIP LEADERS

Young preachers sometimes ask me if I still get nervous before I preach. They are surprised when I readily answer, "Absolutely!" My father used to tell young preachers that the moment we stop getting nervous, we should quit preaching. I used to think that was odd counsel. I understand it much better now.

When I stand to preach, I am very nervous. My nervousness is not because I am unprepared. No matter how prepared I am, standing before the saints on the Lord's behalf makes me acutely aware of my spiritual neediness. Charles Spurgeon walked up to his pulpit repeatedly praying, "I believe in the Holy Spirit." I walk to the pulpit expressing the same sentiment in more urgent terms: "Lord, if You don't help me, nothing good is going to come of this!"

You ask, "Can you preach and pray at the same time?" My answer, "You better!"

The greatness of the ministry task and limitation of my human resources consume me until I pray. Before I start preaching, I publicly pray that the Lord would help me to speak faithfully and the congregation to hear clearly. Then my nerves calm down.

But I continue praying as I preach. You ask, "Can you preach and pray at the same time?" My answer, "You better!"

Multiple things go through the preacher's mind as he preaches. I am not sure the preacher thinks about numerous things simultaneously. Instead, the mind quickly and constantly shifts from one thing to another—consisting of thoughts that are good and bad, true and false, wise and foolish. The preacher can only get through this internal civil war with divine help.

Preaching, or any way you serve God, is a gracious privilege, holy duty, and solemn stewardship. If you don't feel overwhelmed that the Lord would use someone like you to do something as important as this, you shouldn't be doing it. "Not that we are sufficient in ourselves to claim anything as coming from us," Paul confessed, "but our sufficiency is from God" (2 Cor. 3:5).

We access God's help through believing prayer. I believe it happens after prayer! Whatever you need God to do in you, through you, or for you, it happens after prayer. But it also happens as you pray. Leading worship involves more than preaching sermons, offering prayers, reading Scriptures, making music, or managing technology. It involves diligent prayer. Here are three prayer requests you should make as you lead worship (or pray for your worship leaders).

ASK GOD TO GUIDE YOUR THOUGHTS

As you commune with God in private devotion, your mind can be flooded with distractions. If this can happen in what A. Louis Patterson called "the private chambers of your own praying ground," imagine how easily it can happen as you lead worship.

All kinds of mundane thoughts come to your mind as you serve on Sundays. Members walk. Babies cry. Children pass notes.

Deacons sleep. You suspect that person glued to their smart device is not engaged in the worship. You spot guests you have never seen before. You don't see that faithful member in her regular spot. You start thinking about last week. Or you start thinking about next week. The only way to rein in wandering thoughts is to ask God to guide your thoughts.

On rare occasions, something happens in the service that is so distracting that I lose my train of thought. In those moments, I have responded by praying aloud, "Lord, please hold my mind." I secretly and repeatedly utter this petition throughout the message. And I am a witness that God will answer this prayer. God can help you stay focused. God can bring to your memory what you need to remember. God can enable you to disregard vain thoughts.

ASK GOD TO GUARD YOUR HEART

Leading worship requires physical preparation and mental concentration. Moreover, it demands spiritual devotion. It does not matter if your head is in the game, if your heart is not. You should come to the task of leading worship with a prepared assignment, a rested body, and a consecrated heart. Before service, pray with David, "Search me, O God, and know my heart! Try me and know my thoughts! And see if there be any grievous way in me, and lead me in the way everlasting!" (Ps. 139:23–24).

You should examine your heart for any unconfessed sin before you lead God's people in worship. And you should continue the spiritual examination as you lead worship. The worship leader ministers directly to the congregation. Ultimately, the worship leader ministers to an audience of one. First Samuel 16:7 says, "For the LORD sees not as man sees: man looks on the outward appearance, but the LORD looks on the heart."

One of my favorite prayer choruses says, "Lord, I want to be a Christian in my heart." But that is not all that is going on in our hearts. You may not feel good about the message you will preach. You may feel the music is not as prepared as it should be. You may be leading the same people for years who seem to refuse to change. Ask God to guard your heart against fear, worry, or discouragement.

Or it may be the other way around. You may be overconfident about your sermon. You may be thinking about your music set as a performance rather than an offering. You may be insensitive or indifferent toward the spiritual needs of the congregation. Ask God to guard your heart against pride, folly, and carnality.

ASK GOD TO GUIDE YOUR WORDS

I advise preachers to write full sermon manuscripts, whether they use them in the pulpit or not. I think this is one of the most practical things a preacher can do to grow in his preaching. I have a pragmatic reason for advocating sermon manuscripts. The work of thinking through what you want to say in advance helps keep the preacher from filibustering in the pulpit. Even though I have mapped out what I want to say before I get to the pulpit, I still need the Lord to edit in what He wants in and edit out what He wants out.

Words are powerful. That is all the more the case with words of worship. Solomon admonished,

> Guard your steps when you go to the house of God. To draw near to listen is better than to offer the sacrifice of fools, for they do not know that they are doing evil. Be not rash with your mouth, nor let your heart be hasty to utter a word before God, for God is in heaven and you are on earth. Therefore let your words be few. (Eccl. 5:1–2)

Worshipers must be careful with their words when they come before God. How much more does this apply to those who lead worship. "Not many of you should become teachers, my brothers," James counsels, "for you know that we who teach will be judged with greater strictness" (James 3:1). There are severe consequences for those who hear the Word of God without doing what it says. The consequences are more severe for those who teach the Word of God without doing what it says.

And let me be clear. The one who preaches is not the only one who teaches. The one who sings also teaches (Col. 3:16). Those who minister to others by speaking must do so as one who speaks oracles of God (1 Peter 4:11). To speak (or sing) to the glory of God, ask God to guard your tongue against saying anything untrue, unwise, or unhelpful. Pray, "Let the words of my mouth and the meditation of my heart be acceptable in your sight, O Lord, my rock and my redeemer" (Ps. 19:14).

Chapter 30

✝

I WILL NOT OFFER WHAT COSTS ME NOTHING

Several life verses drive the pursuit of faithfulness in my life and labor for Christ. First Timothy 4:16 is one: "Keep a close watch on yourself and on the teaching. Persist in this, for by so doing you will save both yourself and your hearers." Second Timothy 2:15 is another: "Do your best to present yourself to God as one approved, a worker who has no need to be ashamed, rightly handling the word of truth." Second Timothy 4:2 exhorts: "Preach the word, be ready in season and out of season; reprove, rebuke, and exhort, with complete patience and teaching." I regularly share these verses with young ministers who ask for a passage to encourage them in their gospel work.

Another passage reminds me of my duty to give God my best. However, I rarely share this verse with others. It is not a verse from the Pastoral Epistles. It is not even from the New Testament. It is 2 Samuel 24:24: "But the king said to Araunah, 'No, but I will buy it from you for a price. I will not offer burnt offerings to the LORD my God that cost me nothing.' So David bought the threshing floor and the oxen for fifty shekels of silver."

Let me set the scene.

Israel's enemies rose against them. King David responded by counting his fighting men. Scripture describes what happened next in two different ways. First Chronicles 21:1 says, "Then Satan stood against Israel and incited David to number Israel." Second Samuel 24:1 says, "The anger of the LORD was kindled against Israel, and he incited David against them, saying, 'Go, number Israel and Judah.'"

Nothing was inherently wrong with David seeking to know how many fighting men were available. In any other situation, it would be considered the wise thing to do. Jesus asked, "Or what king, going out to encounter another king in war, will not sit down first and deliberate whether he is able with ten thousand to meet him who comes against him with twenty thousand?" (Luke 14:31). Yet David's census was sinful, because Israel was supposed to rely on God and not numbers for military victory. The commander of David's army, Joab, warned him, "May the LORD your God add to the people a hundred times as many as they are, while the eyes of my lord the king still see it, but why does my lord the king delight in this thing?" (2 Sam. 24:3).

The king's advisor was right. Victory would come by divine favor, not military might. Ask Gideon and his small band of fighting men (Judg. 7). God plus one always equals a majority. Joab gave David godly counsel, but the word of the king prevailed. In so doing, David greatly displeased the Lord. When the Lord confronted David, the king confessed, "I have sinned greatly in what I have done" (2 Sam. 24:10). Numbering the people was about more than the size of David's army. It was a statement of faith. Counting the fighting men demonstrated that David was not counting on God.

Israel would suffer the consequences of David's sin. But the Lord permitted David to choose the punishment. David had three options.

Three years of famine in the land. Three months of persecution from
their enemies. Or three days of pestilence. David responded, "I am
in great distress. Let us fall into the hand of the LORD, for his mercy is
great; but let me not fall into the hand of man" (2 Sam. 24:14). God
gave Israel three days of pestilence, and David begged God for mercy
as he saw thousands of his people falling dead.

The Lord graciously restored His fallen leader. God commanded David to offer a sacrifice on the threshing floor of Araunah the Jebusite. David obediently went to the house of Araunah
and asked to buy his threshing floor to build an altar. Araunah was
willing to let David use his threshing floor free of charge. His land
was David's land. "No, but I will buy it from you for a price," David
replied. "I will not offer burnt offerings to the LORD my God that cost
me nothing" (2 Sam. 24:24).

This verse weighs heavily on me as I prepare to lead in worship
from week to week. I know it has nothing to do with worship planning, sermon preparation, or pulpit ministry. Yet it has everything
to do with what we do for the Lord.

David's statement is a call to spiritual excellence. When I speak
of excellence, I am not talking about style points, entertainment
value, or special elements that seek to beat the world at its own
game. By excellence, I mean this: If it bears God's name, it deserves
our best. Of course, what is "best" will look different depending
on the leader, congregation, and situation. As we serve the Lord,
David's standard should be ours: "I will not offer to the Lord that
which costs me nothing."

What should worship cost us?

PERSONAL CONSECRATION

David prayed, "Let the words of my mouth and the meditation of my heart be acceptable in your sight, O Lord, my rock and my redeemer" (Ps. 19:14). This is a good prayer for worshipers to offer. Pray both petitions. The words of our mouth must be acceptable in God's sight. Our worship should proclaim sound doctrine, gospel truth, and a Christ-centered focus. But God is also looking at the meditations of our hearts. The Lord is not honored by true words from a false heart. We must guard our hearts so that the words of our mouth will be the overflow of our devotion to Christ. Pay whatever it costs to preach with a clean conscience, pure heart, and godly motivations.

DILIGENT PREPARATION

Have you heard the one about the preacher who did not prepare? As he stood to preach, he pleaded under his breath, "Lord, please speak to me." The Lord spoke to the lazy preacher and said, "You should have studied!" Upon hearing that story, I concluded that I do not want the Lord to speak to me in the pulpit. Get it? As best I can, I want to be on the same page with the Lord before I enter worship. Of course, the Lord is free to change the plan. But I refuse to use that as an excuse not to prepare myself.

There are worship leaders who make it look so easy. In most instances, they work hard to make it look easy. There is a price to pay to lead in a way that honors God, facilitates worship, and edifies believers. How long does it take to prepare to lead well in worship? As long as it takes. Don't quit until the hard work of preparation is done. If you preach, sing, play an instrument, run media, or lead a worship service in any way, you know what it is to feel that you were not as prepared as you should have been. If you are sincere, humble, and devoted, you do not know what it is to leave the service on Sunday feeling overprepared. Prepare yourself to carry out your ministry responsibilities so you can leave the service and say to God, "I offered You my best today."

BELIEVING PRAYER

You have prepared yourself to lead in worship. You have prepared for the ministry you will render to others in the Lord's name. Very good. But there is another price to pay. It is the cost of believing prayer. In a real sense, you should consider the entirety of the service you render to be an exercise in prayer. Pray as you prepare yourself to serve. Pray before the service begins. Pray as you serve. Pray after your duty is done. Pray for yourself. Pray for the team you will serve with. Pray for those you will minister to in the congregation. Our prayers do not inform God of what He does not already know. Our prayers advertise our dependence upon God.

Pray because the Word of God commands us to pray.

Pray because it is how the Father provides for His children.

Pray because it works! It happens after prayer.

What happens after prayer? Everything. Whatever you need the Lord to do in or through or for you happens after prayer. There is a lot you can do to make a difference after you have prayed. But there is really nothing you can do to make a difference until you have prayed. When we work, we work. When we pray, God works!

> > > ✝ ＜ ＜ ＜

EPILOGUE

I am glad and grateful that you have stuck with me to the end of this book. As you have worked through these sections and chapters, I am sure that you have read portions of this book that you disagree with. I understand. And I do not take your objections personally. I am encouraged that you disagree with me on some of my points and the positions I have taken. It means that you have read this book thoughtfully. Furthermore, it is evidence that you recognize how serious the subject of worship is.

There is room for different perspectives on worship matters. In fact, we should normalize debating this subject without engaging in "worship wars." Our worship of God should be shaped and governed by the Word of God. Sacred Scripture should be foundational to all that happens in our public and corporate worship assemblies. Beyond the foundation, however, God's Word should explicitly structure our worship lives—privately and publicly.

The Scriptures should increasingly shape our worship. Yet let's be honest. Many other factors influence our worship practice. Personal preferences, cultural environments, denominational affiliation—and many other considerations—have formed, reformed, or deformed us. We will never agree on everything when it comes to worship. But I hope your reading of *On Worship* has lifted your gaze beyond mundane, secondary, and worldly thoughts to the ultimate goals of true worship.

That sinners will be saved by the knowledge of God and the saving work of Christ.

That redeemed followers of Christ will grow in the grace and knowledge of Christ, growing up "to the measure of the stature of the fullness of Christ" (Eph. 4:13).

And that, ultimately, the worthy name of our true and living God will receive the glory that is due to Him. May we sing on unending repeat, "Who is like you, O Lord, among the gods? Who is like you, majestic in holiness, awesome in glorious deeds, doing wonders?" (Ex. 15:11). Moses and the people of Israel sang those words after crossing the Red Sea on dry ground and seeing Pharaoh and his armies drown. This miracle of deliverance was wrought by mighty power and the outstretched hand of the Lord.

We have even more reason to praise the glory of God because of the Lord Jesus Christ. By the righteous life, atoning sacrifice, and triumphant resurrection of Jesus, we have been redeemed from the bondage of guilt, delivered from the domain of darkness, and adopted as sons and daughters of the heavenly Father. Paul declared, "To the King of the ages, immortal, invisible, the only God, be honor and glory forever and ever. Amen" (1 Tim. 1:17). May God the Father, God the Son, and God the Holy Spirit be glorified now and forever as we worship Him in spirit and truth!

NOTES

1. Michael P. Green, *1500 Illustrations for Biblical Preaching* (Grand Rapids: Baker Books, 2000), 407–8.

2. A. W. Tozer, *Keys to the Deeper Life,* rev. and expanded (Grand Rapids: Zondervan, 1957, 1984), 87–88.

3. William Temple, quoted in *The Westminster Collection of Christian Quotations,* comp. Martin H. Manser (Louisville: Westminster John Knox Press, 2001), 407.

4. Abraham Kuyper, speech opening the Free University in 1880. Quoted in *Abraham Kuyper: A Centennial Reader,* ed. James D. Bratt (Grand Rapids: Eerdmans, 1998), 461.

5. John Piper, *Let the Nations Be Glad! The Supremacy of God in Missions* (Grand Rapids: Baker, 2010), 15.

6. Warren W. Wiersbe, *Real Worship: Playground, Battle Ground, Holy Ground,* 2nd ed. (Grand Rapids: Baker, 2000), 145.

7. Warren W. Wiersbe, *On Being a Servant of God* (Grand Rapids: Baker, 2007), 23.

8. Bryan Chapell, *Christ-Centered Worship: Letting the Gospel Shape Our Practice* (Wheaton, IL: Crossway, 2017), 160.

9. This language is drawn from Marva Dawn's excellent book, *Reaching Out Without Dumbing Down* (Grand Rapids: Eerdmans, 1995), 75ff.

10. Edmund Clowney, *The Message of 1 Peter* (Downers Grove, IL: IVP, 2021), 72.

11. *Sermons of Rev. C. H. Spurgeon of London* (New York: Funk & Wagnalls Company, 1892), 253.

FOR FURTHER READING

As I mentioned in the introduction, this book is not a comprehensive treatment of the subject of worship. I trust what I have written is rooted in biblical truth. But I have also benefited from the wisdom of others who have written on this important topic. The following is a list of several resources you may find beneficial as you further your study on Christian worship.

D. A. Carson, ed., *Worship by the Book* (Grand Rapids: Zondervan, 2002).

Warren W. Wiersbe, *Real Worship: Playground, Battle Ground, Holy Ground,* 2nd ed. (Grand Rapids: Baker, 2000).

John F. MacArthur Jr., *The Ultimate Priority* (Chicago: Moody, 2012).

Bob Kauflin, *Worship Matters: Leading Others to Encounter the Greatness of God* (Wheaton, IL: Crossway, 2008).

Matt Merker, *Corporate Worship* (Wheaton, IL: Crossway, 2021).

Brian Croft, *Gather God's People: Understand, Plan, and Lead Worship in Your Local Church* (Grand Rapids: Zondervan, 2015).

Ligon Duncan, *Does God Care How We Worship?* (Phillipsburg, NJ: P&R Publishing, 2020).

Bryan Chapell, *Christ-Centered Worship: Letting the Gospel Shape Our Practice* (Wheaton IL: Crossway, 2017).

Phillip Graham Ryken, Derek W. H. Thomas, and J. Ligon Duncan III, eds., *Give Praise to God: A Vision for Reforming Worship* (Phillipsburg, NJ: P&R Publishing, 2011).

Keith Getty and Kristyn Getty, *Sing! How Worship Transforms Your Life, Family, and Church* (Nashville: B&H Books, 2017).

Matt Boswell, *Doxology & Theology: How the Gospel Forms the Worship Leader* (Nashville: B&H Books, 2013).

Marva Dawn, *A Royal Waste of Time: The Splendor of Worshiping God and Being Church for the World* (Grand Rapids: Eerdmans, 1999).

A. W. Tozer, *Whatever Happened to Worship?: A Call to True Worship* (Camp Hill, PA: Wingspread, 2012).

Terry L. Johnson, *Worshiping with Calvin: Recovering the Historic Ministry and Worship of Reformed Protestantism* (Darlington, England: Evangelical Press, 2014).

R. C. Sproul, *The Holiness of God* (Carol Stream, IL: Tyndale, 2000).

MORE FROM H.B. CHARLES

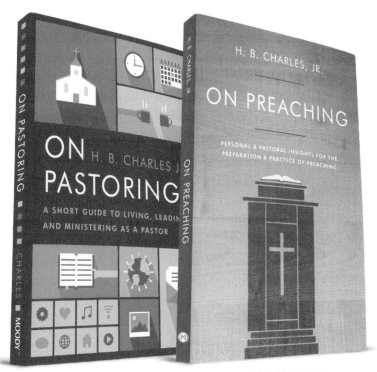

978-0-8024-1460-1   978-0-8024-1191-4

also available as eBooks

DON'T JUST EXPLAIN THE BIBLE.
LET YOUR PEOPLE FEEL ITS PASSION.

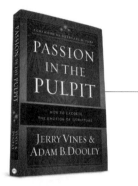

Jerry Vines and Adam Dooley teach you how to exegete not only the verbal content of Scripture, but also its emotional appeal. Learn the exegetical steps to discern the pathos of your text. Master the verbal, vocal, and visual techniques to communicate it with power and emotion. And start preaching not only to your people's minds but also to their hearts.

978-0-8024-1838-8

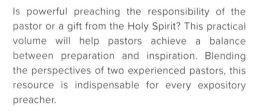

Is powerful preaching the responsibility of the pastor or a gift from the Holy Spirit? This practical volume will help pastors achieve a balance between preparation and inspiration. Blending the perspectives of two experienced pastors, this resource is indispensable for every expository preacher.

978-0-8024-1557-8

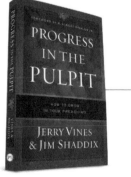

While most preaching books are geared toward new preachers, *Progress in the Pulpit* builds on the basics and focuses on aspects of preaching that often fall into neglect. It also gives special attention to some of the latest cultural and homiletical trends that many pastors don't have time to research on their own.

978-0-8024-1530-1